Overcoming ————
LANGUAGE
———— Barriers

Overcoming LANGUAGE Barriers

How Teachers Can Help Dialect Speakers Succeed

AMANDA J. JONES, Ed.D.

authorHOUSE®

AuthorHouse™
1663 Liberty Drive
Bloomington, IN 47403
www.authorhouse.com
Phone: 1-800-839-8640

Published by AuthorHouse   05/06/2013

ISBN: 978-1-4772-9045-3 (sc)
ISBN: 978-1-4772-9044-6 (hc)
ISBN: 978-1-4772-9046-0 (e)

Library of Congress Control Number: 2012921740

TABLE OF CONTENTS

LIST OF TABLES

ACKNOWLEDGEMENTS

This book would not be complete without acknowledging those who played pivotal roles in making this vision become a reality. First, I would like to thank God through our Lord Jesus Christ for granting me the determination to complete this book.

I truly appreciate the English/language arts teachers across the United States who took the time to share their thoughts and classroom experiences regarding this topic. I extend gratitude to the many linguists, educators, and other student advocates whose works contributed not only to educational research but also to the progression of dialect speakers. Finally, I thank my family and loving parents, Bishop and Mrs. A. J. Jones, Sr., who have shown unconditional love and support throughout my entire life.

AUTHOR'S PREFACE

This book is the result of a research project in which I randomly selected English/language arts teachers across the United States to complete surveys regarding their perceptions of students' use of Black English dialect. I chose this panel of teachers with the presumption that they would provide valuable feedback because of their direct association with Standard (or Academic) English instruction and the language arts classroom. Results from the study provided much insight. However, one of the most intriguing findings was the elevated level of candor regarding survey participants' feelings of inadequacy with respect to Black English, its speakers, and African American culture.

As Carol Myers-Scotton (2006) advises, one should not "assume all African Americans are speakers of this dialect just because they're African American . . . it's a socially based dialect, not an ethnically based dialect, and many African Americans are speakers of the standard dialect" (p. 28). However, when discussing the most appropriate means of assisting those who speak Black English, educators essentially focus on African American learners because the dialect is most commonly associated with this ethnic group. Therefore, the purpose of this book is twofold: (a) to serve as a springboard for those who possess an ardent desire to understand foundational concepts regarding Black English dialect and African American learners and (b) to provide readers with data regarding English/language arts' teachers' perceptions of Black English usage based upon the author's research study. Although some attention is given to examples of linguistic features of Black English commonly used in mainstream classrooms, the book's purpose is not to provide a compendium of all Black English features. Rather, the book presents a synthesis of literature and research enveloping major topics in Black English dialect as well as practical means of perpetuating success among linguistically different students and learners in general.

INTRODUCTION

CROSS-CULTURAL COMMUNICATION

The United States of America embodies many different cultures and continues to grow in multiplicity, complexity, and therefore, uncertainty. In response, people continually seek ways to reach a common goal of working harmoniously among all cultural groups. However, the attainment of this goal is contingent upon the ability to effectively communicate while interacting both verbally and nonverbally from culture to culture.

Effective communication in the United States means, in part, mastering the mainstream language most widely accepted in society, or the Standard English language. Gail Tompkins (2003) noted that the English language involves four cueing systems which people use while reading, writing, listening, and speaking: (a) phonological, (b) syntactic, (c) semantic, and (d) pragmatic. The first three cueing systems involve the use of sound, structure, and meaning, respectively. The phonological system is associated with the spelling of approximately 44 sounds in the English language. The syntactic system focuses on how words are combined to form sentences, while the semantic system focuses on meanings of words (pp. 7-8).

The characteristics of the first three cueing systems in the English language are relatively straightforward and tend to invoke minimal controversy. However, it is the pragmatic system that seems to open the door to much debate. The pragmatic system involves the social and cultural uses of language in which people use language varieties (or dialects) based on their social class, ethnicity, and geographical regions. Therefore, learning the role that culture plays in communication is fundamental as mainstream speakers work to build *communicative competence* (ability to comprehend and use utterances appropriately) among dialect speakers. Being aware of both linguistic and social uses of language may enhance one's *mutual intelligibility*, which is defined as the ability of speakers of different languages to readily understand each other without much effort (Myers-Scotton, 2006).

The Value of Culture and Communication

Cultural awareness has become perhaps one of the most widely discussed topics in education. As schools continue to serve students from multicultural backgrounds, educators search for meaningful ways to better communicate with these students and cater to their diverse learning styles. Because students of varied cultures have different ways of communicating, it is particularly important to become knowledgeable about students' culture and language varieties in order to accommodate differences.

Culture Defined

Culture refers to a group or community with which people share common experiences that shape the way they relate to the world (LeBaron, 2003). Lustig and Koester (2003) defined culture as a learned set of shared interpretations about beliefs, values, and norms which affect the behaviors of a relatively large group of people. Culture pertains to groups in which people are born such as gender or national origin as well as groups to which they join themselves (e.g., social connections).

Anthropologists Avruch and Black (1993) purported that culture provides the "lens" by which people view their world, the "logic" by which they order it, and the "grammar" by which it makes sense (p. 33). Essentially, culture centers upon what people see, how they make sense of what they see, and how they express themselves. Spring (2004) maintained that one must understand culture in order to truly understand communication.

Communication Defined

Communication represents a channel whereby people attempt to understand the world around them. LeBaron (2003) maintained that communication is the vehicle by which meanings are conveyed, identity is composed and reinforced, and feelings are expressed. It represents the intermingling of social acts within a complex cultural milieu, reflecting the way in which people live and interact with their world. When communicating, different groups of people from various cultures seek ways to make sense of their world. In making sense of their world, they attempt to gain an understanding of who they are, where they fit in, and what contributions they are able to make in society. People hold diverse values and ideologies; therefore, it is important to find ways to communicate effectively with others of varying cultures.

Sociolinguistics and Language Variation

Throughout history, language has served as a bridge on one hand and perhaps a barrier on the other. Language is important for basic interpersonal communication as well as self-directed language tasks including speaking, reading, and writing (Ball & Farr, 2003; Green, 2002; Jax, 1988). Ball and Farr (2003) referred to language as the abstract system underlying the entire speech and writing behavior of a community. Smitherman (2000) added that language represents the "foundationstone [sic] of education and the medium of instruction in all subjects and disciplines throughout schooling" (p. 119). Regardless of how one defines language, however, it is diversity within languages that seems to receive considerable attention among linguists and other scholars.

In 1952, Haver C. Currie coined the term *sociolinguistics*, which focused on the social functions of speech. Chambers (2002) defined sociolinguistics as "the study of the social uses of language" (p. 3). The field of sociolinguistics focuses on the manner in which communicative competence and speech community come together: the entire linguistic, dialectal, and stylistic range from which language users make their choice (Pride, 1979). Although sociolinguistics has been the focus of numerous studies, Chambers (2002) maintained that the most productive studies during the four decades of sociolinguistic research have concentrated on the social evaluation of linguistic variants.

According to Reagan (2005), language diversity exists not only with respect to different distinct languages but also in terms of variation within particular languages. Research supported the position that variation in language is a natural reflection of cultural and community differences (Labov, 1972, 2001; Osborn & Osborn, 2005; Smitherman & Baugh, 2002). Scott and Machan (1992) maintained that language variation refers to the reality that individual speakers modify their

3

language patterns according to specific factors such as topic discourse, social relationships, written or spoken communication, and the size and nature of the audience and setting. Ball and Farr (2003) noted that within each community, a variety of language codes and ways of speaking vary according to the levels of different languages, regional and social dialects, registers, and channels of communication. However, inherent in these varied modes of interaction are opportune moments for effective communication or sometimes unintended occasions of vast confusion.

Each thread of cultural fabric contributes to an amalgam of interconnected values. Therefore, becoming educated about a particular culture is essential in order to understand how to relate to it. Knowing how to adequately serve diverse students involves understanding the meaning of culture and communication as well as how they are both intricately tied to language. Becoming familiar with the cultural and social uses of language may enhance not only one's communicative competence but also one's mutual intelligibility across cultures.

Black English Usage in Mainstream Society

In 1979, James Baldwin posed a question in the title of his article, "If Black English Isn't a Language, Then Tell Me, What Is?" While his message seemed clear, today's pressing question may not necessarily ask whether Black English is a language, but rather, "Is Black English a language that will help promote success in mainstream society?"

Much discourse encompassing Black English has focused on whether African Americans' use of the dialect impeded communication with other cultural groups and stifled opportunities for success in various social and professional endeavors. Notable scholars and researchers agreed that Black English, the dialect that numerous African American students speak, may actually impede access to important social networks in the wider, mainstream society (Craig & Washington, 2002; Delpit, 1995; Oubre, 1997; Smitherman, 2000).

Advocates of Black English contended that African American students should be afforded the opportunity to learn and speak a language rooted in their culture, while others recognized the stigma inherent in its usage (Ball, 1997; Baugh, 2000; Boone, 2003; Dandy,

4

1991; Seymour et al., 1999; Williams, 2001). Delpit (1995) explained that:

> To imply to children or adults . . . . that it doesn't matter how you talk or how you write is to ensure their ultimate failure. I prefer to be honest with my students. I tell them that their language and cultural style is unique and wonderful but that there is a political power game that is also being played, and if they want to be in on that game there are certain games that they too must play . . . . When I speak, therefore, of the culture of power, I don't speak of how I wish things to be but of how they are. (pp. 39–40)

Delpit (1995) maintained that while students should be proud of their heritage, they should understand that "real power" lay in their ability to master Standard English because the most socially valued dialect will inevitably enjoy a privileged status (p. 274). In other words, being able to effectively communicate with Standard English speakers will give them the competitive edge to succeed in mainstream society.

Consider the controversy surrounding Senator Harry Reid's comments regarding President Barack Obama during the 2008 presidential campaign. In their book, *Game Change*, John Heilemann and Mark Halperin (2010) quoted Reid, stating that he predicted then-Senator Barack Obama could become the first Black President of the United States because he was "light-skinned" with "no Negro dialect, unless he wanted to have one" (p. 37). Reid's remarks were perhaps intended to commend Mr. Obama for his effective communication skills. However, some critics called for Reid's resignation. In response, Reid apologized for his "poor choice of words" and for "offending any and all Americans, especially African Americans . . ." (Preston, 2010, p. 1). Prior to that incident, then-Senator Joseph R. Biden, Jr. offered an apology for telling the New York Observer that Mr. Obama was "the first mainstream African American who is articulate and bright and clean . . ." (Horowitz, 2007). One might ask, "Should one become offended at such comments or reflect upon the veiled lesson to be learned from these comments?" (*I leave it to the reader to answer this question.*)

In a society rife with competition in the workplace, a vacillating economy, and African American students who continue to trail their counterparts in academia (Aud, Fox, & KewalRamani, 2010; Ogbu, 2003), educators search for ways to overcome barriers to the educational attainment and success of this student population. However, educators may find that their attempts will only be futile without first endeavoring to break down barriers to effective communication.

In subsequent chapters, the reader is introduced to various topics regarding Black English and dialect speakers. Chapter one chronicles controversies and opposing views surrounding the dialect, while chapter two documents the educational experience of African Americans and the influence of culture on student learning. In chapter three, the author expounds upon research findings from the abovementioned research project regarding English/language arts (ELA) teachers' perceptions of Black English usage. Chapter four presents additional research-based and culturally sensitive practices to assist diverse learners. The final chapter discusses next steps in the mission to catapult success for all students.

CHAPTER ONE

BLACK ENGLISH IN RETROSPECT

Chapter Overview

Black English dialect is commonly known as *Ebonics*, a term which Robert Williams coined in 1973 to represent a combination of the terms *ebony* (meaning black) and *phonics* (denoting sound). However, over the past few decades, the dialect has acquired several nomenclatures such as African American Language, Black Language, African American Vernacular English, and African American English (Smith & Crozier, 1998; Smitherman & Baugh, 2002; Rickford & Wolfram, 2009). Ball (1998) characterized Black English as having highly consistent pronunciation, grammar, and lexicon, which many lower and working class African American youth in the United States learn as a first dialect. Bland-Stewart (2005) offered another description of Black English, defining it as the systematic, rule-governed dialect of Standard English that is spoken among some (but not all) African Americans as well as others who are not African American.

This chapter presents key historical accounts concerning the evolution of Black English and controversial issues surrounding the dialect. The chapter also illustrates opposing views regarding whether Black English speakers possess deficits or differences with respect to language usage. The chapter concludes with a snapshot of some of the most common features and rules of Black English dialect and why teachers should familiarize themselves with such concepts.

Theoretical Geneses of Black English

During the time Africans arrived in North America, much linguistic diversity existed between ancestral West African languages and the developing American English language. Africans' geographic location and social situation defined their varying modes of interaction. They spoke different native languages and possessed different levels of proficiency in English (Wolfram, 2000; Wolfram & Beckett, 2000).

According to Wolfram (2000), the synchronic and diachronic significance of Black English has undergone more scrutiny than any other vernacular variety. However, after decades of research on Black English, no consensus existed on how the language had evolved. Wolfram maintained that in the 1950s and early 1960s, dialectologists accepted the Anglicist hypothesis that Black English derived from British-based dialects. In the 1970s, a creolist hypothesis replaced the Anglicist theory. The creolist hypothesis suggested that Black English originated in creolized languages stemming from the African Diaspora (Bailey, 1965; Dillard, 1972).

According to the National Endowment for the Humanities (2005), several theories of Black English derivation emerged. However, two extant theories tended to supersede others. One theory suggested that when slaves of different language backgrounds were transported from Africa to America, they developed a pidgin (or a simplified version of a language) used to communicate among people or groups who did not share a common language. A second theory posited that African American slaves in the South learned English from indentured servants (frequently of Scots-Irish descent) who spoke nonstandard English. Black English was a language whose origins began in a colonial displacement of people, cultures, and languages of West Africa. As a result, many Standard English speakers considered Black English to be an unacceptable variant of standard American English (Ziegler & Osinubi, 2002).

Controversial Issues Surrounding Black English

Throughout history, much controversy has enveloped the use of Black English dialect. One of the most pivotal moments in the history of

Black English occurred in 1979, when the so-called Black English Trial brought into question teachers' perceptions of what they considered to be the socially accepted form of English. Another debacle later ensued involving the California Oakland School Board and their decision to use Black English dialect in their school curriculum. These occurrences involving Black English usage in schools gained the attention of not only court officials but also linguists, educators, parents, policymakers, and others who held a vested interest in the public school system.

The Black English Trial

In the 1979 legal court case, Martin Luther King Junior Elementary School Children v. Ann Arbor School District, parents in Ann Arbor, Michigan brought a suit against the Ann Arbor school district. Plaintiffs alleged that the Black elementary students spoke a version of Black English as their home language that inhibited their equal participation in the instructional programs; however, the school had not taken appropriate action to overcome the barrier. Plaintiffs asked the court to intervene on the children's behalf to protect them from becoming functionally illiterate. In order to accomplish this task, the plaintiffs asked the court to require the Ann Arbor School District Board to take appropriate action to teach the students to read in the Standard English of the school (University of Michigan Digital Library [UMDL], 2004).

Key contributors. Linguists, educators, reading specialists, and psychologists testified during the trial proceedings. These and other experts provided grammatical and historical evidence regarding the evolution of Black dialects (Baugh, 1998; Mufwene, Rickford, Bailey, & Baugh, 1998; Sealy-Ruiz, 2005; Smitherman, 2000). The presiding judge, Judge Charles Joiner, based his decision primarily on the expert testimony of notable linguists such as William Labov, J. L. Dillard, Dan Fader, and Geneva Smitherman (Baugh, 1998; National Council of Teachers of English [NCTE], 1982; Smitherman & Baugh, 2002).

Ann Arbor court decision. In its decision, the court found that a language barrier existed which impeded the teachers' attempts to teach Standard English to Black English speakers. The court ruled that teachers who spoke Standard English needed to recognize and accept the nonstandard dialects of their students. The court determined that insensitive teachers who treated the children's language system as inferior could cause a barrier to students' ability to learn to read and use Standard English (Crawford, 2005).

The court noted that teachers who are unfamiliar with the linguistic features of their students' nonstandard dialects may either intentionally or unintentionally cause students to become insecure about their home language. Consequently, students may feel that teachers of Standard English reject not only their nonstandard dialect but also its speakers (NCTE, 1982). Judge Joiner directed the Ann Arbor School District Board to provide a plan to assist the teachers in overcoming the language barrier (UMDL, 2004). In response to the ruling, the district devised a year-long training plan in language diversity for the teachers at the school, which the court approved (Smitherman & Baugh, 2002).

The Oakland Controversy

In 1996, over 15 years following the Black English trial, the California Oakland School Board adopted a resolution to incorporate the use of Ebonics, or Black English, in their educational curriculum. The board concluded that language was the primary deterrent to Black English-speaking students' success (Ball & Farr, 2003). The Oakland Board consented to regard Black English as a second language to obtain eligibility for bilingual funds for their Black English-speaking student population (Knapp, 1996).

The school board based their decision on the premise that the proposal would better meet the needs of their African American students who had comprised 71% of their special education population but only 53% of the entire district population (Knapp, 1996). This decision immediately spawned national attention among millions of Americans via newspapers, radio, and television (Seymour et al., 1999; Williams, 2001). According to Green (2002a), because of misunderstandings surrounding the Oakland Board's proposal, the media reported false claims that educators would begin teaching Black English to children in the Oakland School District. The result was a tumultuous wave of dissent.

Political leaders, educators, and parents voiced strong sentiment against the school board's proposal, stating that the move would yield greater detriment to the students' learning (Rickford & Rickford, 2000). Although the school board's intent was to improve African American students' academic performance, the public's response prompted the school board to amend portions of their proposal.

Black English Dialect: Deficit or Difference?

Over forty years ago, William Labov (1970) maintained that the fundamental goal of the school was to teach reading and writing of Standard English. In a seminal study of language variation, Labov (1972) provided a sociolinguistic theory of language that underscored the importance of teachers recognizing Black English vernacular as a variation of Standard English. He disputed the claim of Bereiter and Engelmann (1966), who suggested that nonstandard English was a verbal deprivation. Although advocates of Black English have attempted to promote authenticity and respect for the language, others have questioned the legitimacy of the dialect (Bereiter & Englemann, 1966; Machan & Scott, 1992).

Deficit Theory

Deficit theory, or verbal deprivation theory, suggested that lower working-class, ethnic minority children were not equipped to succeed at school because of their deprivation in intellectual development (Stubbs, 1980; Witkosky, 2005). Deficit theorists argued that because of genetic inferiority, African Americans were unable to excel at the same level as White students (Thompson, 2004). With respect to language arts, deficit theory implied that Black English speakers' linguistic deficiencies inhibited them from excelling in the subject. Supporters of deficit theory agreed that students struggling with language arts would be unable to learn a second language and would become even more confused in English if introduced to another language (Fox & Johnson, 2005).

11

Linguists' Response to Deficit Theory

In response to deficit theorists' ideologies, many sociolinguists have sought to denounce linguistic deficit theory as a fallacy directed toward dialect speakers. Labov (1972) resolved that verbal deprivation theory was detrimental to our educational system and would preclude schools from fully realizing their goal. Linguists emphasized that many speakers and teachers of Standard English often viewed nonstandard English as pathological. Scholars concurred that dialectal or language variation involved differences, not deficits (Baugh, 1998; Heck, 1999; Smitherman, 1981; Wolfram, Adger, & Christian, 1999). Smitherman (2000) added that not simply one form of Standard English existed but rather "varieties of standard English—formal, informal, and colloquial" (p. 145).

Intricacies of Dialect: Examples from Black English

During the 1960s and 1970s, research relating to the rules and structural composition of Black English (BE) burgeoned. Throughout that time, several linguists endeavored to dispel the "erroneous linguistic and psychological assertion" that the language variety was evidence of cognitive deficiency in African American people who spoke the dialect (Smitherman & Baugh, 2002, p. 8). Linguists maintained that the many varieties of English, or nonstandard English dialects, consisted of logical and highly structured linguistic systems. However, many Standard English (SE) speakers' concomitant views of inferiority often challenged linguists' assertions (Hoffman, 1997; Smitherman, 1977, 2000).

The field of sociolinguistics has provided some accounts of how Black English speakers have shared certain linguistic features with speakers of Standard English. Black English speakers used nonstandard English features more frequently, however, and the greater differences between Standard English and Black English occurred in the grammar. Numerous linguists agreed that Black English represents a distinct dialect with a fully developed, rule-governed structure subsumed under grammar, phonology, and lexicon. According to linguists, these domains created obstacles in both oral and written communication (Bland-Stewart, 2005; Burling, 1973; Craig & Washington, 2004; Koch, Gross, & Kolts, 2001; Van Sertima, 1971). Green (2002a) suggested that Black

12

English dialect shared similar patterns and lexical items contained in mainstream English; therefore, Standard English speakers often assumed that BE speakers were misusing Standard English constructions. As a result, some linguists recognized the need for teachers to become knowledgeable of BE features in order to best instruct speakers of the dialect (Baugh, 2000; Rickford & Rickford, 2000; Smitherman, 2000).

Familiarizing oneself with foundational Black English speech patterns is perhaps one of the most important catalysts for enhancing one's cultural sensitivity toward Black English speakers. Mainstream teachers should recognize the differences of linguistically diverse learners and work to increase their level of communicative competence with these students. Green (2002a) explained that understanding the rules of Black English usage may lessen the possibility that educators will harbor negative attitudes toward the dialect and its speakers. Christenbury (2000) posited that one of the most challenging "issues for English teachers is their responsibility to students who speak what is considered 'nonstandard' English . . ." (p. 202). Smitherman (2000) added that having the knowledge and acceptance of dialect features may enable language arts teachers to better assist Black English speakers with their reading performance. For example, Smitherman suggested that a BE speaker who reads the sentence, *"The boy needs more money,"* as *"De boy need mow money"* has neither a perceptual/vision problem nor coding/decoding linguistic one. Rather, the dialect speaker has translated the sentence into "good Black English." In this example, the Black English speaker produced homophonic pairs: (a) then/den [initial /th/ pronounced as /d/] and (b) more/mow [*more* pronounced as *mow*] (p. 354).

Past research on language variation identified specific linguistic features evidenced in BE speakers' oral and written expressions. Numerous features characterize Black English; however, the following examples expound upon some of the most frequently used Black English attributes as per research literature: (a) verbal or aspectual markers, (b) phonology (i.e., consonant cluster reduction, substitution of /str/ for /skr/, substitution of voiced /th/ for /d/ and /t/, substitution of voiceless /th/ for /f/ or /v/), (c) copula absence, (d) negative concord, and (e) subject-verb disagreement. These dialect features formed the basis for the author's research study.

Verbal/Aspectual Markers

Verbal forms in Black English dialect have been a central focus of study because they showed marked differences from other English varieties (Ball, 1997; Green, 1999, 2002b; Mufwene et al., 1998). These verbal forms included, but were not limited to, the Black English speakers' use of habitual *be*, aspectual *BEEN*, and the verbal marker *done*.

Habitual be. In Standard English, speakers use adverbs to tell when something occurs habitually. However, BE speakers employ the aspectual or habitual *be* to indicate that something is ongoing (Ball & Farr, 2003; Smitherman, 2000). In situations where Standard English speakers use adverbs such as *sometimes* or *usually*, BE speakers may typically use habitual *be*.

The development of habitual *be* is of particular importance because scholars cited it as often contributing to miscommunication between teachers and BE-speaking students (LeMoine, 2001; Seymour et al., 1999; Smitherman, 2000). For example, as cited in Smitherman's (2000) book, *Talkin' that Talk,* Noma LeMoine reported the following verbal exchange between a teacher and a student:

> "Bobby, what does your mother do?" the teacher asked.
> "She *be* at home," Bobby replied.
> "You mean she is at home," the teacher said.
> "No she ain't," Bobby offered, 'Cause she took my
>   grandmother to the hospital this morning."
> The teacher snapped. "You know what I meant.
> You aren't supposed to say, 'She be at home.' You
> say, "She is at home."
> But Bobby, incredulous, could only reply, "Why
> you trying to make me lie? She ain't at home." (p. 25)

In this scenario, "She be at home" appeared to be an incorrect variation of "She is at home." However, a semantic difference exists between the statements. In Black English, "She *be* at home," means a habitual state referring to ongoing status, whereas "She *is* at home," refers to the present or what is happening now. Smitherman (2000) offered another example where aspectual *be* resulted in a misunderstanding between a teacher and BE-speaking student:

> SCENE: *First grade classroom, Detroit*
> Teacher: Where is Mary?
> Student: She not here.
> Teacher: (exasperatedly): She is *never* here!
> Student: Yeah, she be here.
> Teacher: Where? You just said she wasn't
> here. (p. 25)

In this example, the child inferred that Mary is *usually* present, but she was not present that particular day. However, the teacher's statement, "She is never here," was inaccurate, signifying a lack of knowledge relative to the meaning of aspectual *be* in Black English.

Aspectual BEEN. Aspectual *BEEN* represented another inhibitor to effective communication between mainstream speakers and Black English speakers. Aspectual *BEEN* is capitalized to denote BE speakers' use of stress on the word *been*. In Black English, aspectual *BEEN*, when stressed, typically exemplifies the remote past. Consider the question, "Is she married?" If a BE speaker's response to this question is "She *BEEN* married," the reply conveys that the person had been married for a long time. On the other hand, if no stress is placed on the word *been* it is possible that the person did marry but may no longer be married (Green, 1998, 2002a; Smitherman, 2000). One who is not familiar with the meaning of aspectual *BEEN* may fail to understand the distant past that the term implies.

Aspectual done. Another feature indicative of Black English is aspectual *done*. The BE speaker utilizes the unstressed form of *done* to signify that an event is over. The unstressed *done* is "distinguished from the main verb *done* by pronunciation" (Green, 2002a, p. 686). The BE speaker who states, for example, "He *done done* [sic] his assignments," means that he has *already* done his assignments. The verbal marker unstressed *done* indicates that the event took place in the past and is now over. The term *done* represents a resultant state marker.

15

Phonological Features

According to Stockman (1996), differences in phonology have been distinctively evidenced in dialect differences. Since the 1960s and early 1970s, linguists viewed the phonological differences of Black English and Standard English as contributors to the reading difficulties and standardized test inequities some African American students faced (Bailey & Thomas, 1998; Smitherman, 2000). Past research showed that the phonological differences between Black English and Standard English posed potential risks for Black English speakers learning to read. For example, some phonological processes are not readily perceived in pronunciation (e.g., bald/ball). Therefore, such differences in pronunciation could result in challenges for Black English speakers as they learn to read words with similar sound-spelling correspondences (Fasold & Wolfram, 1970; Labov, 1972, 1995).

Consonant cluster reduction. Consonant cluster reductions in Black English (BE) are evident when BE speakers reduce word-final consonant clusters. In Black English, speakers tend to delete the final member of consonant clusters at the end of words (Bailey & Thomas, 1998). For example, Black English speakers drop certain members of the cluster such as /k/ and /t/ in the words *desk* and *post*. As a result, these speakers pronounce the words as /des/ and /pos/, respectively (Green, 2002a; Smitherman, 2000).

Other examples of consonant cluster reduction are evidenced in BE speakers' use of past tense markers. In this case, BE speakers generally drop the *-ed* in words when referring to past events. For example, in the sentence, *"They walked to the store,"* BE speakers reduce *walked* to /walk/. Here, the BE speaker may realize that the event occurred in the past. However, the BE speaker may simply drop the ending consonant cluster because of his/her acquired dialect (Delpit, 1995, p. 58).

Substitution of /str/ for /skr/. In Black English, speakers may often replace the syllable /str/ with /skr/ when speaking. Green (2002a) asserted that BE speakers followed a specific pattern in which they substituted /str/ with /skr/ when /str/ occurred at the beginning of a word or at the beginning of a syllable. For example, when the initial sound occurred in words such as st<u>r</u>eet and st<u>r</u>ong, BE speakers may have pronounced the words as sk<u>r</u>eet and sk<u>r</u>ong, respectively. This type of substitution also occurred when /str/ was situated at the beginning of a syllable within a word but not necessarily at the beginning of the word (e.g., de<u>str</u>oy [SE] vs. de<u>skr</u>oy [BE]).

Substitution of /th/ for /t/, /d/, /f/, and /v/. The voicing value has played a major role in the production of /th/, /t/, /d/, /f/, and /v/ in Black English dialect (Green, 2002a). One feature in Black English involved interdental fricatives. *Interdental* implies a sound which is articulated by placing the tongue between the teeth, as in the word *th<u>is</u>*. *Fricatives* refer to sounds which are articulated with almost a complete closure, but with just enough of an opening to create turbulence in the airflow. When located at the beginning of a word, Black English speakers pronounce the interdental fricative, voiceless /th/ as /t/. For example, the word *thin* becomes /tin/ and *thigh* becomes /tie/. In contrast, the /d/, /f/, and /v/ sounds substitute the voiced *th* found in Standard English. Where voiced /th/ occurs in Standard English, BE speakers use /d/. For example, the word *these* (SE) becomes *dese* (BE). When located in the word medial position or word final position, the interdental fricative /th/ becomes /f/. For example, the word *bathroom* becomes /bafroom/ and the word *bath* becomes /baf/, respectively. Where voiced /th/ occurs in mainstream English, the voiced *v* may occur in word medial position in Black English. For example, BE speakers may pronounce *brother* as *brova* (Green, 2002a; The Language Samples Project, 2001).

Other Common Features

Linguists have identified other features that are common among Black English speakers. Some of the most frequently noted Black English features include copula absence, negative concord, and subject-verb disagreement.

Copula absence. One well-known feature of Black English is the absence of the copula, or "to be" verbs such as *is* and *are*. This feature has been commonly associated with Black English dialect. Black English speakers often deleted the verbs *is* and *are*, as in the following examples: "*She glad;*" "*They sad*" (Seymour et al., 1999). As shown in the previous example in which the BE-speaking student told the teacher, "*She not here,*" the student omitted the verb *is* and used a variation of the Standard English sentence, "*She is not here.*"

Negative concord. Negative concord, also known as multiple negation and pleonastic negation, has been cited as another well-known characteristic of Black English and many other varieties of English. Negative concord occurred in sentences where speakers used two or more negative morphemes to communicate a single negation (Martin & Wolfram, 1998). For example, in cases where a Standard English speaker might say, "I don't have a car," speakers of Black English might say, "I don't have no car." Where Black English permitted more than one such morpheme in a negative sentence, Standard English used one and (optionally) one or more negative polarity items (NPIs) (e.g., any): "*She didn't want no candy*" (Black English version) vs. "*She didn't want any candy*" (Standard English version).

Subject-verb disagreement and suffix -s. According to Martin and Wolfram (1998), unlike Standard English, Black English invariably showed no subject-verb agreement, except for present-tense finite *be*. In cases where the morpheme *-s* or *-es* would be expected in Standard English, BE speakers omitted the morpheme altogether. For example, in third person singular phrases such as, "He *runs* fast," BE speakers might say, "He *run* fast." Other instances where morpheme *-s* would be omitted occurred in the use of possessives. When using possessives, for example, BE speakers might say, "I saw *mommy* hat," instead of "I saw *mommy's* hat." For words in which suffix *–s* is needed to form plurals, the BE speaker might omit the suffix *–s* altogether (e.g., *poster* vs. *posters*).

Black English Features in Student Writing

Sociolinguistic studies have predominantly focused on spoken language; however, some scholars have studied how writing also reflects language, social contexts, and culture. In an early study of Black English speakers' writing, Whiteman (1976) found that BE speakers frequently used features that differed from Standard English. These features included Black English speakers' use of verbal *–s*, plural *–s*, consonant cluster *–ed*, and forms of the verb *be*. Smitherman (2000) examined results from the National Assessment of Educational Progress from 1984-1988 to explore African American students' use of Black English features in their written essays. Smitherman found that all essays for all years showed an increase in Black English features regarding irregular verbs and subject-verb-agreement-past. Ball and Farr (2003) later cited habitual *be* as being a particular feature evidenced in BE speakers' writing. Ball (1998) suggested that recognizing how patterns of students' spoken language are reflected in written texts is one key principle that underlies the successful evaluation of students' writing.

African Americans and Cultural Conflicts

Timothy Reagan (2005) suggested that the acquisition of socially appropriate oral and written language forms is one of the principal goals of the educational experience. Scholars maintained that in order for teachers to understand their nonstandard English-speaking students and achieve the basic goals of education, they must first gain an understanding of the students' nonstandard language (Cazden, 1996; Labov, 1970; Smitherman, 2000). However, the educational plight of many African American students who speak Black English (BE) dialect has raised concern about a lack of understanding among mainstream teachers and Black English-speaking students. The consequence of such misunderstandings may be significant when considering that countless African American children speak a variety of English which conflicts with the socially accepted, middle-class language (Baugh, 1998; Bland-Stewart, 2005). Some scholars contended that this conflict affects nearly every facet of the children's educational experience as they learn the oral and written forms of the socially accepted dialect of mainstream schools (Seymour, Abdulkarim, & Johnson, 1999).

Various sociolinguists argued that a major contributor to the educational plight among African Americans lay in dialect differences (Ball, 1992; Labov, 1970, 2001; Rickford, 1999; Seymour et al., 1999; Smitherman, 2000; Yates, 1998). Baugh (2000) asserted that teachers and speech pathologists misdiagnosed BE-speaking students because of inadequate training in linguistics (the study of language). Consequently, educators inappropriately placed many linguistically diverse learners in special education. Williams (2001) contended that African American children are crowded into remedial education classes because many of them have never been taught variations of the printed word.

The dismal performance of some African American students may also result from a lack of minority teachers in the classroom. Spring (2002) maintained that poor academic achievement among minority students resulted from a cultural clash that existed between a predominantly White teaching staff and high percentages of cultural minorities. Spring noted that 91.8% of public school teachers were White, whereas only 0.03% of the teachers were African American. However, 35.8% of the students were African American.

Fordham (1996) and Goto (1997) postulated that some African American students deliberately concealed their intellectual abilities to avoid being isolated from their ethnic friends who were not as proficient in school. This type of withdrawal may have resulted when students felt compelled to make a choice between academic success and cultural identity (Gay, 2000; Valenzuela, 1999). Ball and Farr (2003) attributed African Americans' low literacy levels to school classrooms in which communicative systems not only differed but also conflicted. During reading and writing instruction, many African American students may face a conflict between their own cultural linguistic systems and those of mainstream, Standard English systems. African American students may feel a sense of obligation to their own culture, thus resulting in conflicts between some White teachers and African American students (Delpit, 1998; Ogbu, 2003).

Bland-Stewart (2005) resolved that teachers must understand the cultural and linguistic context of a child's behavior and language when testing and observing the student to determine whether or not a learning problem truly exists. Teachers who become more knowledgeable of and sensitive to Black English dialect and African American culture may begin to witness a subjugation of cultural clashes rather than culture.

Teacher Attitudes, Dialects, and Self-fulfilling Prophecies

For years, teacher attitudes have been recognized as important contributors to students' academic success or failure. Studies of social support have suggested that perceptions of supportive teachers are inextricably linked to student outcomes (Ferguson, 1998; Rist, 2000;

Weinstein, 2002; Wentzel, 1997; Youngs & Youngs, 2001). However, if teachers harbor negative attitudes toward students, they may find that any efforts to maximize student achievement will be futile, regardless of what strategies they employ. With respect to language-minority children, Valdes (2001) found that teachers' attitudes and beliefs play a critical role in determining the educational outcomes for these students. Teachers who held negative views toward language-minority students, or who upheld fallacies surrounding their education, often failed to meet the students' academic needs.

Although teacher attitudes may have a direct impact on student performance, the attitudes of school leaders also have the potential to indirectly impact student outcomes. Levine and Lezotte (2001) focused on ways in which school administrators influenced teacher attitudes. They identified the principal, or school leader, as the most decisive factor impacting school effectiveness for English language learners. These scholars maintained that administrators who held positive attitudes toward linguistic and cultural diversity infused their positive attitudes among teachers. As a result, teachers and schools were more equipped to accommodate cultural and linguistic differences.

Attitudes toward language are associated with whether educators view students' dialects as either deficits or differences (Baugh, 2000; Bronstein, Dubner, Lee, & Raphael, 1970; Smitherman & Baugh, 2002). In a study of how Black English dialect and teacher attitudes influenced classrooms, Edwards (1997) found that teachers had failed to support their students' home language and held low expectations for the students' achievement. Consequently, the students failed to reach their fullest academic potential. Smitherman and Baugh (2002) contended that negative perceptions of nonstandard English reflect the belief that vernacular dialects are linguistically inferior to Standard English. They asserted that harboring low expectations for children is deleterious because it conveys a sense that the children are inadequate. Once teachers inculcate beliefs of inadequacy in the minds of children, feelings of inferiority may surface, and children may be more likely to view themselves as self-fulfilling prophecies (Delpit, 1995; Good & Brophy, 2003; Nieto, 1996).

Self-fulfilling prophecies involve situations in which teachers communicate positive or negative academic expectations to students via unconscious or conscious attitudes and behaviors. In response, students conform to the expected behavior, causing the teacher's expectation to become a reality. Teachers who anticipate failure typically hold lower expectations for students, provide insufficient information and feedback, and engage in behaviors that result in student failure. In contrast, teachers who hold high expectations generally expect more from the students, provide greater input, and give students consistent feedback (Tauber, 1997).

Rickford (1999) noted that teachers who lacked knowledge of their students' cultural background imposed detrimental effects on their achievement. Some linguists and scholars attributed pathological views of Black English dialect to the dearth of linguistic understanding among educators (Baugh, 2000; Bland-Stewart, 2005; Smitherman, 2000). They maintained that teachers should not view Black English dialect as a deficit. Rather, teachers should view the dialect as a difference and support linguistically different students in a classroom environment infused with cultural sensitivity and effective teaching practices. Such practices may ultimately "create a fundamental change in teacher attitude toward the student" (Wheeler & Swords, 2006, p. 54).

Chapter Summary

Black English represents perhaps one of the most controversial topics in African American history. While there may be no consensus among scholars regarding the origin of Black English, the reality is that many African American students continue to speak this dialect. Whether difference or deficit, the question remains whether Black English usage advances or inhibits the success of those who speak the dialect. Becoming familiar with common Black English features may assist mainstream speakers in their quest to build their level of communicative competence with speakers of this dialect. On the other hand, failure to do so may inevitably result in cultural conflicts. The next chapter focuses on the educational trends of African American students, the influence of culture on their academic performance, and how teachers may improve the classroom experience for many of these students through culturally sensitive practices.

CHAPTER TWO

AFRICAN AMERICANS IN THE CLASSROOM

Chapter Overview

For decades, African American students' academic performance has paled in contrast to their peers, leaving educators and researchers often searching for solutions to narrow the achievement gap. Although many African American students have succeeded in school and beyond, much attention is given to the overwhelming majority of those who have not been as successful. Becoming familiar with the culture and learning preferences of African American students is an important precursor to effectively teaching and reaching this student population. This chapter addresses such topics, capturing a review of literature and research data regarding the educational trends, academic achievement, and cultural characteristics of African American students. The chapter discusses the importance of culturally responsive pedagogy and offers suggestions for infusing culturally sensitive practices in the mainstream classroom.

The Educational Experience of African Americans

The achievement gap between minority and White students has occupied the forefront of educational statistics for years (Coe, 2006; Jencks & Phillips, 1998; Miller, 1995). Despite countless efforts to narrow the achievement gap, vast disparities have persisted. Compelling evidence showed that students from disadvantaged minority groups achieved poorer outcomes at every level (Education Trust, 2003; Ogbu, 2003; Steele, 1997).

Educational and psychological research has consistently shown that students from disadvantaged U.S. minority groups, particularly African Americans, tended to achieve lower rates of academic success than their White counterparts. Although not all-inclusive, some of these poorer outcomes often involved special education overrepresentation, lower standardized test scores, higher dropout rates, and lower college attendance rates.

Special Education Overrepresentation

In years past, numerous minority children have experienced being relegated to slower educational tracks and special education classes at alarming rates. Yet, an under-representation of minority and low socioeconomic students has existed in gifted and talented programs. This under-representation was especially apparent in the case of African American males, who were least likely to be enrolled in gifted programs (Edwards, McMillon, & Turner, 2010; Ford & Harris, 1999; Seymour et al., 1999). Spring (2002) maintained that African American students comprised only 11% of the total U.S. school population; yet they represented over 14% of the students in special education. The Commission on Behavioral and Social Sciences and Education [CBASSE] (2002) corroborated these findings, citing an unequivocal disproportion in special education in the United States: approximately 5% Asian/Pacific Islander students, 11% Hispanics, 12% Whites, 13% American Indians, and over 14% African Americans.

Aud, Fox, and KewalRamani (2010) reported similar statistics from data collected from 1998 to 2007. According to the report, the percentages of 6- to 21-year-old students who were served under the Individuals with Disabilities Education Act (IDEA) were slightly lower for each of these subgroups. However, African American students maintained the highest percentage when compared to other students: 5% Asians or Pacific Islanders, 9% Hispanics, 8% Whites, and 12% African Americans.

The U.S. Commission on Civil Rights (2009) reported that over 50% of African American students read at below-proficient levels in contrast to slightly over 20% for White students. The authors suggested that African American students' low achievement levels in reading may help explain their overrepresentation in special education. The report cited that "70% to 89% of all referrals to special education implicate poor reading as a first or second reason for the referral" (p. 63).

Reading Achievement and Standardized Test Scores

The achievement gap in standardized test scores among minorities and Whites continues to be a long-standing concern for educators. However, the widest achievement gap has been most evident among African Americans and their White peers (Berlak, 2001; Jencks, 1972; Ogbu, 2003; Osborne, 2001). In fact, with respect to reading achievement, the Education Trust (2003) reported that by the end of high school, African Americans' reading skills were tantamount to those of White eighth-grade students.

National Assessment of Educational Progress reading scores.
Since 1969, the National Assessment of Educational Progress (NAEP) has served as a nationally representative assessment of U.S. students' knowledge and ability relative to reading and other subject areas. The NAEP reports average scores and percentages of 4th, 8th, and 12th grade students performing at or above three levels of achievement, including Basic, Proficient, and Advanced levels (National Center for Education Statistics [NCES], 2010).

In 2005, the NAEP reported that 4th grade African American students scored an average of 200 points in contrast to 4th grade White students (229). A significant achievement gap was also evident in 8th grade students' scores, with African Americans' average score being 243 whereas White students averaged 271 points. The 2007 reading tests showed that 4th grade African American students scored an average of 203 points in contrast to that of 4th grade White students (231). At the

8th grade level, African American students' average score was 245 while White students averaged 272 points.

By 2009, NAEP reading scores were based on a new framework which replaced the framework used from 1992 through 2007. Yet, test scores still resulted in similar outcomes between African American and White students. NAEP 2009 test results indicated that 4th grade African American students scored an average of 205 points in contrast to 4th grade White students' average of 230 points. For 8th grade students' scores, African Americans averaged 246 points, and White students averaged 273 points (U.S. Department of Education, 2009a; U.S. Department of Education, 2009b).

The achievement gap has also persisted between African American and White students at the high school level. In 1992, 12th grade White students scored an average of 297 points in contrast to African American students' average score of 273 points, reflecting a 24-point achievement gap. In 2009, nearly 20 years later, 12th grade White students scored 296 points, scoring higher than their African American peers (269), revealing an even higher achievement gap of 27 points (NCES, 2011).

Scholastic Aptitude Test verbal scores. The 2001 Scholastic Aptitude Test (SAT) results illustrated a recurrent achievement gap between White students and their minority peers. Data showed that SAT averages rose for almost all racial ethnic groups between 1991 and 2001. However, average verbal SAT scores for White students increased from 518 to 529 over a span of 10 years, whereas improvements for African Americans increased from 427 to 433, reflecting an even wider achievement gap (i.e., 91-point gap vs. 96-point gap).

In 2004, African American students, on average, scored 98 points lower on the verbal portion of the SAT test than White students (House, 2006). In 2005, a nearly 100-point achievement gap was evident in national SAT reading scores of African Americans (433) and Whites (532) (Wisconsin Department of Public Instruction, 2005). By 2008, average scores for White students (528) still remained approximately 100 points higher than African American students' scores (430) in critical reading (NCES, 2010). These statistics suggested that since 1991, average reading scores for Whites increased by 10 points (i.e., 518 points in 1991 vs. 528 points in 2008), whereas reading scores for

27

African Americans increased by only three points (i.e., 427 points in 1991 vs. 430 points in 2008). That is, the nearly 100-point achievement gap still lingered despite decades of educational research and discourse surrounding the mission to close the achievement gap.

High School Graduation Rates and College Readiness

Stark disproportions have also been evidenced in the percentage of racial and ethnic groups of students who completed high school and were eligible for college admission. Greene and Winters (2005) noted that a wide disparity was evident between the graduation rates of African American and White students in particular. Greene and Winters noted that, in 2002, about 78% of White students graduated from high school with a regular diploma, in contrast to 56% of African American students. Aud, Fox, and KewalRamani (2010) reported that of the students who entered high school during the 2003–04 school year, 74% graduated within 4 years: 91% of Asians, 80% of Whites, 62% of Hispanics, 61% of American Indians/Alaska Natives, and 60% of Blacks" (p. v). All of these subgroups outpaced Black students.

African American and White students have also differed relative to the number of them who graduated college-ready. Greene and Winters (2005) reported that of those students who graduated from high school in 2002, approximately 40% of White students were prepared for college, whereas 23% of African American students graduated college-ready. By 2008, about 44% of White students aged 18 to 24 were enrolled in colleges or universities in contrast to 32% for Black students (Aud et al., 2010). Ferguson (2006) suggested that the requirements to graduate from high school are set lower than the requirements to apply to a four-year college, leaving many African American high school graduates ineligible to enroll. Ferguson noted that, of those students who enrolled as first-time students at a four-year institution in the 1995-1996 academic year, approximately 62% of White students had completed a bachelor's degree by 2001, in contrast to 43% of African American students.

The NCES (2009b) issued a more recent educational attainment report of persons 25 years and older, which showed how the percentage of Whites (30%) with a bachelor's degree or higher almost doubled that of Blacks (16.8%) between 2005 and 2007. A different report by the

NCES (2009a) reflected that Whites had earned 71.8% of bachelor's degrees conferred for the 2007-2008 school year compared to only 9.8% for Blacks. The NCES (2011) reported strikingly similar statistics for the 2008-2009 school year for Blacks (9.8%) and Whites (71.5%).

Culturally Responsive Pedagogy

Following the beginning of the new millennium, Spring (2002) described the United States as becoming increasingly diverse and expressed how that it was experiencing one of the most dramatic shifts in its racial and ethnic composition. As U.S. schools continue to serve a proliferation of students from culturally and linguistically diverse backgrounds, it is the responsibility of teachers and educational leaders to accommodate these cultural and linguistic differences. Because most teachers will likely teach students of different cultures, it makes sense to focus much attention on the linguistic varieties that permeate U.S. classrooms.

In order to cater to diverse needs, educators must recognize the importance of exercising equitable (not equal) practices in order to provide a quality education for all students. Equitable practices allow for creative, non-traditional instructional approaches that meet individual needs, whereas *equal* practices suggest perfunctory or one-size-fits-all approaches. However, teachers who are under-trained and lack sufficient knowledge of how to teach culturally and linguistically diverse learners may fail to adequately serve these students (Darling-Hammond, 2000a; Nieto, 1999; Villegas & Lucas, 2002).

Educators who view students' cultural and linguistic diversity as deficits rather than differences may often misclassify students as learning disabled (Baugh, 2000; Hoover & Collier, 1985; Minow, 2010; Weismantel & Fradd, 1989). Such misclassifications of minority students may shed light on contributors to the unremitting achievement gap, including why so many of these students are disproportionately relegated to special education classes. Minow (2010) maintained that once these students have been identified as disabled, they are "much more likely to be separated from the mainstream classroom and to have inadequate and inappropriate services as well" (p. 81).

As our world continues to grow in complexity, the changing demographics of school classrooms warrant continuous learning through professional development opportunities. Many scholars agreed that if teachers are to enhance learning opportunities for students, they must be knowledgeable about the social and cultural contexts of teaching and learning (Banks et al., 2001). Gay (2000) contended that if educators continue to be ignorant of, or impugn, the cultural orientations of ethnically different students, they may persist in imposing academic underachievement upon these students. Teachers may seek ways to expand their knowledge of student culture by reading scholarly articles, books, and professional journals. Some may even choose to enroll in higher education courses or attend educational seminars. All of these approaches allow for varying degrees of professional growth. However, the information teachers receive will be of little value if they do not apply the newly acquired knowledge in the classroom.

Snow, Burns, and Griffin (1998) resolved that regardless of what methods teachers employ, quality instruction represents the best weapon against failure. Moje and Hinchman (2004) maintained that providing African American students with high-quality instruction means that all classroom practices need to be culturally responsive in order to represent best practice. Gay (2000) defined culturally responsive pedagogy as utilizing cultural knowledge, frames of reference, past experiences, and learning preferences of ethnically diverse students to make learning more relevant to students. Ladson-Billings (2001) insisted that becoming culturally aware as a teacher is imperative in order for students to experience success.

Culturally responsive teaching involves purposely responding to the needs of culturally and ethnically diverse learners in the classroom. It establishes a connection between the necessary knowledge found in school curriculum and the knowledge derived from student experiences (Brown, 2004; Freire, 1998; Nieto, 1999). Teachers who are culturally responsive embrace the belief that culturally and linguistically diverse learners excel academically when their language, culture, and experiences are valued and used to enhance their learning. Fox and Johnson (2005) concurred that culturally responsive teachers employ instructional approaches based on the premise that culture lies at the heart of student learning. These teachers recognize and accept the glaring reality that each child brings different cultural values, behaviors, experiences, and knowledge into the classroom. Teachers capitalize on the students' prior knowledge and cultural experiences while allowing them to learn and apply what they learn in meaningful contexts. When teachers select instructional content that is meaningful to students and address their unique learning styles and intelligences, students may become more actively engaged in the learning process.

Classroom management also plays an important role in culturally responsive classrooms. In a study to determine whether urban teachers' professed classroom management strategies matched culturally responsive teaching, Brown (2004) found that educators used several management strategies that reflected culturally responsive pedagogy: (a) creation of caring communities, (b) establishment of business-like learning environments, (c) use of culturally and ethnically congruent communication processes, (d) demonstrations of assertiveness, and (e) utilization of clearly stated and enforced expectations. Enforcing explicit rules, procedures, and consequences with *consistency* helps to ensure structure and equity. For example, if *any* student breaks a particular rule, the consequence should be the same for everyone. Maintaining consistency is important not only in maximizing classroom management but also in building trust. When students feel teachers are fair, the channel of communication may widen and allow for more openness and motivation among all students.

Maxim (2006) determined that the overarching goal of culturally responsive education is to gradually and cumulatively empower students through an understanding and appreciation of cultural diversity. All cultural groups possess a system of behaviors, customs, beliefs, and attitudes, which contribute to the diverse makeup of American society. As a result, every student arrives at school with varying ethnic identities, and educators are faced with the responsibility of accommodating these diverse students through culturally responsive pedagogy. Becoming familiar with topics such as linguistic variations and learning modalities may enhance professional growth, improve cross-cultural interactions, and ultimately improve academic achievement for all students.

Learning Preferences of African American Students

African American students inquire and respond in ways that are often different from other students in mainstream classrooms. For this reason, scholars contended that teachers must possess a genuine appreciation for the valuable repertoire of experiences African American

31

students bring to school (Ball, 1997; Ford, Obiakor, & Patton, 1995; Gay, 2000; Nieto, 1999; Smitherman, 2000). Berry (2003) noted that teachers must create some continuity between the learning preferences of African American students and the culture of the school.

Many theorists and educational researchers have long advocated replacing teacher-centered pedagogy with student-centered instruction (Ball, 1997; Costa & Lowery, 1985; Edens, 2000; Hansen & Stephens, 2000). Yet, despite much research and educational discourse supporting the need for teachers to shift from traditional styles of teaching to creative, student-centered approaches to learning, teacher-centered instruction has often permeated many classrooms (Schmoker, 2006). Bennett (2001) suggested that pedagogy, coupled with an understanding of African American cultural style, maximizes student learning. In light of the persistent achievement gaps found between African Americans and other student subgroups, teachers may benefit from research surrounding the learning preferences of many African American students. Over twenty years ago, A. Wade Boykin (1986, p. 244) identified nine dimensions of the African American cultural experience that included the following concepts:

1. Spirituality—the belief that supreme forces influence people's everyday lives.

2. Harmony—the suggestion that humankind and nature are harmoniously interrelated.

3. Movement—an emphasis on pattern, rhythm, music, and dance.

4. Verve—a propensity for relatively high levels of stimulation and excitement.

5. Affect—an emphasis on emotions, feelings, and nurturing.

6. Communalism—a commitment to and awareness that social bonds and responsibilities transcend individual privileges.

7. Expressive individualism—the cultivation of a distinct personality and a proclivity for spontaneous and genuine personal expression.

8. Orality—the use of oral modes of communication to share stories and information.

9. Social perspective of time—viewing time as a social aspect marked by human interaction and by the event shared by others.

Nieto (1999) noted that such elements are often missing, downplayed, or disparaged in mainstream classrooms. Incompatibilities surfaced between African American students' cultural styles and the learning environment in most schools. Nieto argued that the problem was not that their cultural styles were incompatible with learning. Rather, the problem lay in the reality that most classrooms do not value these styles as legitimate conduits for learning. Kendall (1996) averred that it is the responsibility of the teacher to determine the preferred learning style of each child in the classroom and plan accordingly. Kendall explained that the initial step in identifying a child's learning style is to observe the various ways in which the child interacts in a learning environment.

In her book, *Other People's Children*, Lisa Delpit (1995) discussed survey findings relating to the teacher/learning preferences of White, African American, and other minority learners. All groups of students responded to a question of whether they preferred to learn new concepts from teachers, books, friends, or computers. Delpit found that more African American learners preferred to learn new concepts from *human* teachers, whereas White students preferred learning from computers. This discovery supports Boykin's (1986) claim regarding the affect or nurturing aspect of the African American cultural experience. Shade and Thomas (1997) concurred that African American students were inclined to have a preference toward a relational style of learning, characterized by freedom of movement, variation, creativity, divergent thinking, inductive reasoning, and focus on people.

McIntyre and Battle (1998) surveyed over 300 students served in emotionally and/or behaviorally disordered (EBD) programs regarding their perceptions of good teachers. The study examined four teacher trait clusters: (a) personality traits, (b) treatment of students, (c) behavior management practices, and (d) instructional skills. The results indicated that, in contrast to their White peers, African American students perceived *personality traits* and [respectful] *treatment of students* as being more important than other traits. In addition, McIntyre and Battle (1998) found that in contrast to views from their White counterparts, African American students viewed caring, relaxed, humorous, and entertaining teachers as being more favorable. Similarly, Sanacore (2004) found that African American children tended to thrive in classrooms that were caring, cooperative, and community-oriented.

African Americans' Oral Expression and Speech Acts

Over fifteen years ago, Kochman (1990) compared the oral forms of expression of African Americans and Whites, suggesting that the two groups possessed different styles of oral expression. Kochman asserted that whereas the oral expression of White people tended to be more modest and emotionally restrained, African Americans' expression used more of an emotional and involving mode to energize and excite their audience. Smitherman (1998a) characterized African American communication styles as a manifestation of the verbal form of the African American experience.

Smitherman (2000) explained that speech acts in African American culture essentially infer that communication succeeds or fails as a result of the intended and received effects of a message. For example, one speech act unique to African American culture includes *signification*. Signifying represents an African American discourse style, requiring the encoding of messages that involve the use of innuendoes and double meanings (Ball & Farr, 2003). In *signification*, the speaker generally deploys put-downs, insults, and exaggeration directed toward the listener. Both the listener and the speaker understand that the insults or exaggerations are wittingly used to effectively deliver meaning in message or simply for enjoyment. Each speaker continues to direct the remarks toward the other, until their audience determines a winner (Sealey-Ruiz, 2005; Smitherman, 2000).

One of the more popular styles of oral communication in African American culture is *call-response*. Call-response has been most evident in classrooms with African American learners (Asante, 1998; Foster, 2002; Smitherman, 1977). Gay (2000) characterized the call-response communicative style as a situation in which the speakers make statements while the listeners respond in some expressive form as the speakers are talking. The speakers make *calls* and the listeners make *responses* of affirmation or resistance. Here, the listeners do not wait for an authority to grant permission to speak. When a speaker says something that triggers a response (whether positive or negative), African American listeners are likely to *talk back*. By *talking back*, they gain "participatory entry" to signal speakers that their purposes have either been accomplished or that it is time to change the conversation (p. 91). Foster (2002) noted that the call-response technique originated in religious tradition and is utilized for instructional purposes in some classrooms composed of African American students.

Boone (2003) conducted an ethnographic study of the communicative impact of *call-response* within an African American college classroom. She found that the performance of African American speech acts in the classroom did not serve as a detriment to students' learning. Instead, it yielded greater appreciation of cultural values. Although the call-response technique is indicative of African American cultural value, many teachers who were unaware of this cultural style may have viewed the students as being inconsiderate, disruptive, rude, and speaking out of turn. As a result, the teachers may have reprimanded the students (Gay, 2000). Some researchers emphasized that teachers' rejection of ethnically different students' communication styles may cause students to perceive the rejection as a rejection of the students' humanity, and therefore, promote risks of academic failure (Delpit, 1988; Ogbu, 2003).

Cultural Sensitivity and Constant Correction

Correcting students during classroom instruction is certainly no new concept in education. Oftentimes, teachers correct students who mispronounce or misspell words during reading or writing instruction. Although they may have good intentions, teachers who constantly correct students may actually impede rather than promote students' progress. In an effort to promote greater success among English language learners, various scholars have insisted on the avoidance of constant correction (Cunningham, 1976; Delpit, 1995, 2006; Snow & Kamhi-Stein, 2006). Coelho (2004) argued that constant correction of English language learners may yield negative effects, discouraging, rather than encouraging student learning.

In an early study of African American first graders, Ann McCormick Piestrup (1973) found that teachers who constantly interrupted their Black English-speaking students to correct them produced the lowest-scoring and most unresponsive readers. In contrast, teachers who built on the students' language produced the highest-scoring and most enthusiastic readers. About three years later, Cunningham's (1976) findings reiterated a similar theme in her study of teachers' correction responses to Black English dialect miscues. Cunningham observed that 189 teachers from four different geographic regions corrected 78% of the dialect-specific translations, considering them as errors.

Delpit (2006) reported similar observations in which teachers constantly corrected students each time they mispronounced words during reading instruction. She argued that this method of teaching simply undermined the reading process, causing students to feel inept and lose the entire purpose of reading as a meaning-making experience. Rather than constantly correcting students, teachers model effective communication. Modeling effective communication is particularly important for Standard English language learners because it reinforces what is taught in the classroom without demeaning students. Coelho (2004) explained that errors, or dialect miscues, are a natural part of the language-acquisition process and that teachers should use constructive ways of teaching, such as privately discussing language differences to avoid humiliation.

Teachers should be proactive by diagnosing students' challenges early on, plan and modify instructional practices, and monitor student progress regularly. Creating a chart and simply taking time to listen and take note of students' use of specific Black English features may facilitate this process. For example, once classroom teachers become familiar with their students' use of specific Black English features, they may employ a practical tool such as the author's S.O.F.T. evaluation tool to monitor students' informal language usage (see Figure 2.1).

36

Black English Features	Assessment Week __6__					
	Mon.	Tues.	Wed.	Thurs.	Fri.	Score
Habitual Be (e.g., She be)	||||	||||	|||	|||	|||	17 (F)
Missing Verb (e.g., He sad)	||||	|||	||||	|||	||||	18 (F)
Subject-Verb Disagreement	||	|||	|	||	|	9 (O)
Possessives (missing -'s)	||	|||	||	|	||	10 (F)
Double Negatives	|	|	||	|	|	6 (O)
Substitution ('d' for 'th')	|||	||	||	|||	||	12 (F)
Substitution ('f' for 'th')	|		|		|	3 (S)
Past Tense (missing -ed)	|	|	||	|	|	6 (O)

Scoring Key:	Based on formal observations and/or written products:
	S—Students **seldom** spoke and/or wrote using the BE
Seldom: S	feature during formal instruction (i.e, 1-4 tally marks).
Occasionally: O	O—Students spoke and/or wrote using the BE feature only **occasionally** during formal instruction (i.e., 5 -9 tally marks).
Frequently: F	F—Students spoke and/or wrote using the BE feature **frequently** during formal instruction (i.e., 10 or more tally marks).
Terminated: T	T—Students have **terminated** spoken and/or written use of BE features during formal instruction (i.e., 0 tally marks).

NOTES: **Alyssa, Brian — Double Negatives**

Figure 2.1. S.O.F.T. evaluation tool used to monitor students'
informal language usage during formal instruction

The purpose of the S.O.F.T. tool is to ensure a non-threatening, or *soft,* approach when recording and addressing concerns regarding students' use of informal language in both oral and written communication. This tool may be used while reviewing written work or listening to students during class discussions. The sample shows how teachers are able to monitor specific BE features most frequently used inside the classroom. Simple codes (e.g., S—seldom used; O—often used; F—frequently used; T—terminated use) inform the teacher of specific features to target for whole or small group instruction. The *notes* section allows teachers to take note of features that are often associated with the same students. If there are only a few students who use certain features more frequently than other students, teachers may address those particular features during individual or small group instruction. This method may assist in maximizing instructional time.

Based on the example in Figure 2.1, habitual *be* and missing verbs are the most frequently used Black English features recorded, signifying which features warrant immediate attention. Given their frequency of use, these concepts may be addressed during whole group instruction. Double negatives, on the other hand, are occasionally used; therefore, double negatives may be addressed during individual or small group instruction. The note indicates that Alyssa and Brian could use further assistance in this area. Although the S.O.F.T. tool may be used to monitor students' informal language usage outside the classroom (e.g., on the playground), the primary purpose for using it during formal instruction is to reiterate the importance of using Standard English in formal settings. Teachers may choose to modify this tool to ensure it corresponds to their students' needs.

Contrastive Analysis, Code-switching, and Bidialectalism

In an effort to promote alternative approaches to constant correction of dialect speakers, linguists and scholars have advocated the use of *contrastive analysis* and *code-switching* strategies. Using the contrastive analysis technique, educators teach students the rules of mainstream language in which they identify similarities and differences between Black English and Standard English. Students discover how the grammar of their home language compares and contrasts with Standard English. This technique has been credited for producing favorable student achievement outcomes when used in the classroom (Celious & Oyserman, 2001; Dandy, 1991; Rickford, 1999; Wheeler, 2005; Wheeler & Swords, 2006).

Once teachers have taught students the procedure for contrastive analysis, students may practice *code-switching*. Code-switching is a strategy in which students learn to alter their speech and behavioral patterns to conform to certain social settings. Myers-Scotton and Ury (1977) defined code-switching as the interaction of two or more linguistic varieties. This interaction involves the alternation between two different languages or dialectical shifts within the same language (Flowers, 2000). In effect, students learn to become bidialectal, that is, knowing how to speak Black English when communicating with other Black English speakers and how to modify their speech when conversing with speakers who value Standard English. Ball and Farr (2003) suggested that bidialectalism is one of the most realistically attainable positions needed for diverse students to obtain academic success. In fact, Wheeler and Swords (2006) maintained that African American students outperformed their White peers in Swords' classroom the year she began teaching code-switching lessons.

Code-switching allows speakers of different cultures to communicate successfully while respecting and valuing each other's culture (Celious & Oyserman, 2001; Dandy, 1991). Interestingly, the story of a deaf professor supported the benefit of code-switching even when using sign language. Carolyn McCaskill, a deaf Black professor, gave an account of her experience as a 15-year-old student in 1968 when she and nine other Black students were enrolled in an integrated school for the deaf. She expressed (through an interpreter) how—after watching her White teacher make unfamiliar hand movements for everyday words—she "was dumbfounded" and asked herself, "What in the world is going on?" As a result, she recognized her need to learn American Sign Language (ASL) in order to communicate with her mainstream teacher and peers at school. But, when at home or with friends, she simply switched to the sign language she knew best, or Black American Sign Language (BASL) (Sellers, 2012, p.1).

By learning to code-switch, McCaskill empowered herself to better communicate with different cultural groups by respecting the sign language each group valued. She was able to interact with those who used mainstream sign language without abandoning the sign language that had helped her communicate with family and friends throughout her life.

The purpose for employing contrastive analysis and code-switching techniques is to teach students the importance of using mainstream English in formal settings. Teachers explain this process while also communicating to students that however they speak at home or within informal settings is their choice. As teachers become more knowledgeable of Black English rules and utilize strategies such as contrastive analysis and code-switching, students may be able to better identify differences between Standard English and Black English.

Smitherman (2000) noted that this method of teaching helps circumvent deficit theories and low teacher expectations. For example, if African American students say (or write) "She be at home," instead of immediately correcting or deriding the students, linguistically-informed teachers may engage in meaningful dialogue with students to discuss the statement's meaning and how to speak or write the sentence using Standard English for formal settings.

Chapter Summary

The goal of education continues to focus on providing a quality education for all students and closing the achievement gap between the majority and minority learner. However, standardized assessment data revealed persistent achievement gaps between African American and White student subgroups. Advocates of Black English speakers have called on educators to make concentrated efforts to become more knowledgeable regarding linguistic and cultural differences in order to better meet the needs of African American students and other diverse learners. Teachers who embrace culturally sensitive practices may, in effect, exude positive attitudes and behaviors toward linguistically and culturally diverse learners, communicate higher expectations, and therefore, open avenues for heightened student achievement. The next chapter provides an overview of the author's research study regarding English/language arts teachers' perceptions of Black English usage. The summary outlines both quantitative and qualitative findings from the study.

CHAPTER THREE

A STUDY OF TEACHERS' PERCEPTIONS

Chapter Overview

This chapter presents perceptions of English/language arts teachers, participants in the author's research study whose survey responses greatly contributed to the production of this book. The purpose of the research was to determine the perceptions of English/language arts teachers concerning Black English usage in students' oral and written expression. The information reflects findings for both quantitative and qualitative data obtained from participants' survey responses (Jones, 2007). (See Appendix A for a copy of the survey instrument.)

For researchers choosing to conduct a similar study, the first section provides conceptual definitions and an overview of the sample population, statistical analyses, and validity and reliability of the survey questionnaire. Following this overview is a presentation of data according to: (a) demographic variables for the study, (b) statistical findings relative to specific research questions, and (c) qualitative findings based on participants' responses to open-ended survey questions. Appendix B provides supplements relative to the study's purpose, significance, foundational assumptions, limitations and delimitations, research design, data collection, and analysis procedures. The chapter ends with conclusions based on major findings, implications for educational practice, and recommendations for future research.

Conceptual Definitions

The author/researcher employed specific definitions for the purpose of this study. The conceptual definitions included:

1. Black English- A systematic, rule-governed dialect of Standard English, spoken among some (but not all) African Americans, as well as others who are not African American (Bland-Stewart, 2005).

2. Communicative Competence- The ability to produce socially acceptable utterances which would normally be part of a native speaker's competence in a particular language (Hymes, 1974).

3. Dialect- a language variety associated with a particular regional or social group (Wolfram & Schilling-Estes, 1998).

4. Dialectology- the study of dialects, or the regional and social aspects of language (Shuy, 1967).

5. Grammar- synonymous with sentence structure, usage, and syntax; refers to such things as word order, function words, and grammatical endings (Weaver, 1979).

6. Nonstandard English- any variety of English which deviates from the grammatical structure, pronunciation, idiomatic usage, or word choices associated with educated native speakers of mainstream, or Standard English (Ball & Farr, 2003).

7. Standard English- the middle-class, educated, language variety associated with native speakers of a region (Wolfram & Schilling-Estes, 1998).

Sample Population and Statistical Analyses

The participants for this study reflected a purposive sample of 88 (N = 88) elementary and secondary English language arts teachers across the United States, members of the National Council of Teachers of English (NCTE). The 12.0 version of the *Statistical Package for the Social Sciences* (SPSS 12.0) provided descriptive and inferential analyses of quantitative data. For inferential statistics, the researcher used one-way Analysis of Variance (ANOVA) for data analysis between subjects. In order to compare independent variables that were not proportional, the researcher utilized the Mann-Whitney U test, which is the non-parametric analog to the parametric ANOVA. Using coding and categorization methods, the researcher identified important themes that emerged from participants' open-ended responses, or qualitative data.

Validity of Survey Questionnaire

The researcher revised the survey instrument; therefore, it was necessary to retest the validity of the questionnaire. The validity analyses included Bartlett's Test of Sphericity and the Kaiser-Meyer-Olkin (KMO) measures of sampling adequacy. The validity analyses revealed significance and adequacy for each cluster. The KMO measures included: (a) 0.74 for cluster one (*Communicative Competence Regarding Black English*), (b) 0.54 for cluster two (*Challenge of Teaching Standard English to Black English Speakers*), and (c) 0.82 for cluster three (*Importance of Constant Correction of Black English Usage*).

Principal factor analysis measured the internal validity of each cluster. Three eigenvalues emerged that were greater than one and accounted for over 40% of the variance for each cluster, which indicated a good result. The major eigenvalue accounted for approximately: (a) 57% of the variance for cluster one (*Communicative Competence Regarding Black English*), (b) 46% of the variance for cluster two (*Challenge of Teaching Standard English to Black English Speakers*), and (c) 45% of the variance for cluster three (*Importance of Constant Correction of Black English Usage*).

Reliability of Survey Questionnaire

The researcher ran an additional test of reliability on the final questionnaire because of the survey revisions. The utilization of factor analysis revealed that the overall alpha coefficient for the survey questionnaire was 0.70. This reliability coefficient met Nunnaly's (1978) standard of a satisfactory alpha coefficient of at least 0.70. The reliability coefficients for each of the three clusters included the following: (a) a reliability alpha of 0.82 for cluster one (*Communicative Competence Regarding Black English*), (b) a reliability alpha of 0.69 for cluster two (*Challenge of Teaching Standard English to Black English Speakers*), and (c) a reliability alpha of 0.84 for cluster three (*Importance of Constant Correction of Black English Usage*). Tables 1-3 show the reliability coefficients for each strand:

Table 1.

Cluster One (Communicative Competence Regarding Black English) (N = 88)

Survey items	Alpha if item deleted
8. I am very familiar with Black English (BE) (a non-standard English dialect).	0.86
11. I am able to communicate well with BE-speaking students.	0.76
12. I have a strong rapport with BE-speaking students.	0.75
13. I clearly understand BE-speaking students' colloquial syntax (everyday speech).	0.75
Overall Cluster Reliability	0.82

Table 2.

Cluster Two (Challenge of Teaching SE to Black English Speakers)
(N = 88)

Survey items	Alpha if item deleted
9. I find it challenging to teach writing composition to Black English (BE)-speaking students.	0.65
10. I find it more difficult to teach writing composition to BE-speaking students than other students.	0.63
20. BE-speaking students become frustrated when corrected for incorrect use of Standard English (SE) in writing.	0.59
21. BE-speaking students often become frustrated when corrected for incorrect oral use of SE.	0.64
Overall Cluster Reliability	0.69

Table 3.

Cluster Three (Importance of Constant Correction of BE Usage)
(N = 88)

Survey items	Alpha if item deleted
14. I often correct BE-speaking students' speech during informal discussions (outside of class).	0.81
15. I often correct BE-speaking students' speech during formal/class discussions.	0.81
16. I feel it is necessary to constantly correct BE-speaking students during class discussions.	0.80
17. I feel it is necessary to constantly correct BE-speaking students during writing instruction.	0.82
18. It is important to correct BE-speaking students each time they mispronounce a word during reading time.	0.83
19. I correct BE-speaking students' writing each time they use non-standard English in written composition.	0.83
22. BE-speaking students should be encouraged to use only Standard English at and away from school.	0.82
Overall Cluster Reliability	0.84

Demographic Variables

The demographic variables for the study included ethnicity, highest level of education, gender, years of experience as an educator, academic training in nonstandard English dialects, age, and grade level(s) taught. Frequency tables provided the frequency by percent of occurrences for these independent variables. Tables 4-10 show the frequencies and percentages according to the study participants' demographic variables.

Ethnicity

Study participants' demographic data included diverse ethnicities. However, the non-proportionality of the *ethnicity* variable resulted in the collapsing of data into two ethnic groups: White and non-White. The ethnicity demographic variable showed that 88.6% of the respondents were White, whereas 11.4% were non-White. Table 4 displays the frequencies and percentages for the *ethnicity* variable.

Table 4.

Frequencies for Ethnicity (N = 88)

Ethnicity	Frequency	Percent
White	78	88.6
Non-White	10	11.4
Total	88	100.0

48

Highest Level of Education

The *highest level of education* variable included two levels: bachelor's degree and graduate degree. The *highest level of education* variable showed that 15.9% of respondents obtained only bachelor's degrees, whereas 84.1% of respondents earned bachelor's and graduate degrees. Table 5 provides the frequencies and percentages for the *highest level of education* variable.

Table 5.

Frequencies for Highest Level of Education (N = 88)

Level of Education	Frequency	Percent
Bachelor's	14	15.9
Graduate	74	84.1
Total	88	100.0

Gender

The *gender* demographic variable comprised two levels: female and male. The *gender* demographic variable showed that 80.7% of the participants were female and 19.3% of the participants were male. Table 6 shows frequencies and percentages for the *gender* variable.

Table 6.

Frequencies for Gender (N = 88)

Gender	Frequency	Percent
Female	71	80.7
Male	17	19.3
Total	88	100.0

Years of Experience as an Educator

The *years of experience as an educator* variable consisted of two levels: 1-15 years of experience as an educator and 16 or more years of experience as an educator. The *years of experience as an educator* variable indicated that most respondents (55.7%) had 16 or more years of experience, whereas the remaining respondents (44.3%) had 1-15 years of experience. Table 7 shows frequencies and percentages for the *years of experience as an educator* variable.

Table 7.

Frequencies for Years of Experience as an Educator (N = 88)

Years of experience	Frequency	Percent
1-15 years	39	44.3
16+ years	49	55.7
Total	88	100.0

Academic Training in Nonstandard English Dialects

The *academic training in nonstandard English dialects* variable included two levels: Yes response and No response. The *academic training in nonstandard English dialects* variable showed that the majority of the respondents (59.1%) received no training, whereas 40.9% of the respondents had received training. Table 8 displays frequencies and percentages for the *academic training in nonstandard English dialects* variable.

Table 8.

Frequencies for Academic Training in Nonstandard English Dialects (N = 88)

Academic training	Frequency	Percent
Some training	36	40.9
No training	52	59.1
Total	88	100.0

Age

Teacher's age was a continuous variable that the researcher collapsed into a categorical variable. In categorical form, the *age* variable included three levels: 25-41 years old, 42-56 years old, and 57 years or older. As a continuous variable, the teachers' average age was 47, with a standard deviation of 12, minimum age of 25, and maximum age of 70. In categorical form, 34.1% of teachers were between 25 and 41 years old, 33% were between 42 and 56 years old, and 33% were 57 years old or older. Table 9 shows frequencies and percentages for the *age* variable.

Table 9.

Frequencies for Age (N = 88)

Age	Frequency	Percent
25-41 yrs.	30	34.1
42-56 yrs.	29	33.0
57 yrs. or older	29	33.0
Total	88	100.0

Grade Level(s) Taught

The *grade level(s) taught* demographic variable indicated that respondents taught at varying levels: elementary, secondary, and all levels. However, because of proportionality concerns, normal distribution issues, and sample size factors, the researcher collapsed this variable into two levels: one grade level taught and two or more levels taught. Data indicated that 86.4% of the participants taught only one grade level (elementary/secondary), whereas 13.6% of the participants taught two or more grade levels. Table 10 shows frequencies and percentages for the *grade level(s) taught* variable.

Table 10.

Frequencies for Grade Level(s) Taught (N = 88)

Grade level(s) taught	Frequency	Percent
One level	76	86.4
Two or more levels	12	13.6
Total	88	100.0

Survey Items and Cluster Analyses

Cluster analyses revealed the five highest and five lowest survey items of importance to participants, based on their mean responses. The mean responses on the cluster items are shown in Table 11 (five highest) and Table 12 (five lowest). Table 13 supplies the means for each of the dependent variables or clusters.

Table 11.

Five Highest Ranking Survey Items (N = 88)

Survey items	*n*	*M*	*SD*
8. I am very familiar with Black English (BE) (a non-standard English dialect).	87	2.43	1.06
19. I correct BE-speaking students' writing each time they use non-standard English in written composition.	87	2.63	1.25
13. I clearly understand BE-speaking students' colloquial syntax (everyday speech).	88	2.68	1.01
12. I have a strong rapport with BE-speaking students.	88	2.98	0.91
11. I am able to communicate well with BE-speaking students.	87	3.07	0.97

As shown in Table 11, the highest ranking item of importance focused on ELA teachers' ability to communicate well with BE-speaking students, with which approximately 70% of the participants agreed. The remaining four of the five highest ranking items of importance (in descending order) included participants' perceptions regarding their: (a) strong rapport with BE-speaking students, (b) comprehension of BE-speaking students' colloquial syntax, (c) constant correction of BE-speaking students' use of nonstandard English in writing, and (d) familiarity with Black English dialect.

Table 12.

Five Lowest Ranking Survey Items (N = 88)

Survey Items	n	M	SD
16. I feel it is necessary to constantly correct BE-speaking students during class discussions.	88	0.95	1.02
14. I often correct BE-speaking students' speech during informal discussions (outside of class).	88	1.10	1.09
18. It is important to correct BE-speaking students each time they mispronounce a word during reading time.	86	1.13	1.17
22. BE-speaking students should be encouraged to use only Standard English at and away from school.	88	1.48	1.21
20. BE-speaking students become frustrated when corrected for incorrect use of Standard English (SE) in writing.	86	1.71	0.99

As indicated in Table 12, the five lowest ranking areas of importance included participants' perceptions regarding: (a) constant correction of Black English-speaking students during class discussions, (b) constant correction of BE-speaking students' speech during informal discussions (outside of class), (c) constant correction of BE-speaking students' mispronunciation of words during reading time, (d) reinforcement of only Standard English usage at and away from school, and (e) BE-speaking students' tendency to become frustrated when corrected for incorrect use of Standard English in writing. Approximately 70% of the sample participants disagreed with three survey items in particular (items 14, 16, and 18, respectively): (a) constant correction of BE-speaking students' speech during informal discussions (outside of class), (b) constant correction of BE-speaking students during class discussions, and (c) correction of BE-speaking students each time they mispronounced a word during reading time.

Table 13.

Means and Standard Deviations for Clusters (N = 88)

Cluster	n	M	SD
Communicative competence regarding BE	88	2.79	0.80
Challenge of teaching SE to BE speakers	88	1.91	0.77
Importance of constant correction of BE usage	88	1.62	0.86

As Table 13 shows, the *Communicative Competence Regarding Black English* variable had the highest mean ($M = 2.79$) of the three clusters. Approximately 70% of the sample's responses ranged between ratings of 2.0 and 3.6 on this variable, which suggested that most respondents tended to agree with possessing communicative competence when communicating with BE speakers. The *Constant Correction of Black English Usage* cluster had the lowest mean ($M = 1.62$). Approximately 70% of the participants' responses ranged between ratings of 0.72 and 2.52 on this variable, which suggested that most respondents tended to disagree with constant correction of Black English usage.

Findings According to Research Questions

For this research study, the researcher formulated 11 research questions which examined English/language arts teachers' perceptions of Black English usage in students' oral and written expression. The parametric one-way ANOVA, Tukey's HSD Post Hoc, and non-parametric Mann-Whitney U statistics were useful for inferential data analysis. Data reduction through measures such as coding and categorization allowed for the analysis of qualitative data to identify emergent themes.

Descriptive and Inferential Data Analyses

Seven research questions focused on demographic or independent variables across three clusters: (a) communicative competence regarding Black English, (b) challenge of teaching Standard English to Black English speakers, and (c) importance of constant correction of Black English usage. Survey items 8, 11, 12, and 13 comprised cluster one, *Communicative Competence Regarding Black English.* Cluster two, *Challenge of Teaching Standard English to Black English Speakers,* included survey items 9, 10, 20, and 21. The final cluster, *Importance of Constant Correction of Black English Usage,* contained survey items 14, 15, 16, 17, 18, 19, and 22. (See Tables 1-3 for the organization of the survey clusters.)

Research question one. Is there a difference between English/language arts teachers' ethnicity and their perceptions across the three clusters: (a) communicative competence regarding Black English, (b) challenge of teaching Standard English to Black English speakers, and (c) importance of constant correction of Black English usage? The Mann-Whitney U analysis used White and non-White groups for comparison across each cluster. The Mann-Whitney U test examined central tendency comparisons of the two ethnicity groups because these groups were non-proportional and violated the normal distribution and homogeneous variance assumptions for the ANOVA. Tables 14-19 provide the mean ranks and Mann-Whitney U results for ethnicity across each cluster.

The Mann-Whitney U analysis revealed no statistically significant difference ($z = -1.08$, $p = .28$, two-tailed) in the *Communicative Competence Regarding Black English* ranking between the White ($M_{rank} = 43.46$) and non-White ($M_{rank} = 52.65$) groups. Tables 14-15 show the mean ranks and Mann-Whitney U results for White and non-White respondents relative to the *Communicative Competence Regarding Black English* cluster.

Table 14.

Mean Ranks for Ethnicity by Communicative Competence Regarding Black English (N = 88)

Ethnicity	n	Mean rank
White	78	43.46
Non-White	10	52.65

Table 15.

Mann-Whitney U for Ethnicity by Communicative Competence Regarding Black English (N = 88)

Source	Value
Mann-Whitney U	308.50
Wilcoxon W	3389.50
z	-1.08
Asymmetrical significance (two-tailed)	.28

The Mann-Whitney U analysis depicted no statistically significant difference ($z = -.87$, $p = .39$, two-tailed) in the *Challenge of Teaching Standard English to Black English Speakers* ranking between the White ($\underline{M}_{rank} = 45.34$) and non-White ($\underline{M}_{rank} = 37.95$) groups. Tables 16-17 provide the mean ranks and Mann-Whitney U results for White and non-White respondents according to the *Challenge of Teaching Standard English to Black English Speakers* cluster.

Table 16.

Mean Ranks for Ethnicity by Challenge of Teaching Standard English to Black English Speakers (N = 88)

Ethnicity	n	Mean rank
White	78	45.34
Non-White	10	37.95

Table 17.

Mann-Whitney U for Ethnicity by Challenge of Teaching Standard English to Black English Speakers (N = 88)

Source	Value
Mann-Whitney U	324.50
Wilcoxon W	379.50
z	-.87
Asymmetrical significance (two-tailed)	.39

The Mann-Whitney U analysis showed no statistically significant difference ($z = -1.28$, $p = .20$, two-tailed) in the *Importance of Constant Correction of Black English Usage* ranking between the White ($\underline{M}_{rank} = 43.26$) and non-White ($\underline{M}_{rank} = 53.20$) groups. Tables 18-19 show the mean ranks and Mann-Whitney U results for White and non-White groups with respect to the *Importance of Constant Correction of Black English Usage* cluster.

Table 18.

Mean Ranks for Ethnicity by Importance of Constant Correction of Black English Usage (N = 88)

Ethnicity	n	Mean rank
White	78	43.26
Non-White	10	54.20

Table 19.

Mann-Whitney U for Ethnicity by Importance of Constant Correction of Black English Usage (N = 88)

Source	Value
Mann-Whitney U	293.00
Wilcoxon W	3374.00
z	-1.28
Asymmetrical significance (two-tailed)	.20

The Mann Whitney U analysis indicated no statistically significant difference regarding ethnicity. However, certain trends emerged from the data. Non-White respondents ($\underline{M}$ $_{rank}$ = 52.65) rated the *Communicative Competence Regarding Black English* cluster higher than White respondents ($\underline{M}$ $_{rank}$ = 43.46). In addition, non-White respondents ($\underline{M}$ $_{rank}$ = 54.20) rated the *Importance of Constant Correction of Black English Usage* cluster higher than White respondents ($\underline{M}$ $_{rank}$ = 43.26). These trends suggested that non-White ELA teachers were more likely than White ELA teachers to agree with possessing communicative competence when communicating with Black English speakers. Non-White respondents were also more favorable of constant correction of Black English usage than White respondents.

Research question two. Is there a difference between English/ language arts teachers' age and their perceptions across the three clusters: (a) communicative competence regarding Black English, (b) challenge of teaching Standard English to Black English speakers, and (c) importance of constant correction of Black English usage? As a categorical variable, teacher's age consisted of three levels: 25-41 years old, 42-56 years old, and 57 years old or older. One-way analysis of variance (ANOVA) tested the difference in sample means for age. Tables 20-26 show the means, standard deviations, and ANOVA results for age with respect to each cluster.

Results from the ANOVA analysis displayed no statistical significance in the sample means for age on the cluster, *Communicative Competence Regarding Black English.* Although the *p* value was near .05 on this variable, the ANOVA results revealed no statistical significance, $F(2, 88) = 2.84, p = .06$. Tables 20-21 display the means, standard deviations, and ANOVA results for teacher's age relative to the *Communicative Competence Regarding Black English* cluster.

Table 20.

Means and Standard Deviations for Age by Communicative Competence Regarding Black English (N = 88)

Age	*n*	*M*	*SD*
25-41 yrs.	30	2.63	.86
42-56 yrs.	29	2.68	62
57 yrs. or older	29	3.07	.83
Total	88	2.79	.80

Table 21.

Analysis of Variance for Age by Communicative Competence Regarding Black English (N = 88)

Source	*SS*	*df*	*MS*	*F*	*p*
Between groups	3.46	2	1.73	2.84	.06
Within groups	51.68	85	.61		
Total	55.14	87			

Results from the ANOVA analysis displayed no statistical significance in the sample means for age on the cluster, *Challenge of Teaching Standard English to Black English Speakers*, $F(2, 88) = 2.20$, $p = .12$. Tables 22-23 display the means, standard deviations, and ANOVA results for teacher's age in relation to this cluster.

Table 22.

***Means and Standard Deviations for Age by Challenge of Teaching
Standard English to Black English Speakers (N = 88)***

Age	*n*	*M*	*SD*
25-41 yrs.	30	2.11	.76
42-56 yrs.	29	1.91	.72
57 yrs. or older	29	1.70	.79
Total	88	1.91	.77

Table 23.

***Analysis of Variance for Age by Challenge of Teaching Standard
English to Black English Speakers (N = 88)***

Source	*SS*	*df*	*MS*	*F*	*p*
Between groups	2.51	2	1.26	2.20	.12
Within groups	48.59	85	.57		
Total	51.10	87			

The ANOVA analysis revealed statistical significance within the variable, *Importance of Constant Correction of Black English Usage*, $F(2, 88) = 5.32$, $p < .05$. Initially, the origin of significance was unknown because three levels were subsumed under the *Importance of Constant Correction of Black English Usage* cluster. In order to determine the origin of statistical significance, the researcher utilized Tukey's honestly significant difference (HSD) Post Hoc test for analysis.

Results from the Tukey test indicated that statistically significant differences were between 25-41 year-olds and 42-56 year-olds at the $p <$ .05 level. Findings suggested that all age groups tended to disagree regarding the *Constant Correction of Black English Usage* cluster. However, 25-41 year-olds were less apt to disagree ($M = 1.93$) than 42-56 year-olds ($M = 1.24$) and those who were 57 years or older ($M = 1.69$). Tables 24-25 show the means, standard deviations, and ANOVA results for teacher's age for the *Constant Correction of Black English Usage* cluster. Table 26 shows results from Tukey's HSD analysis.

Table 24.

Means and Standard Deviations for Age by Importance of Constant Correction of Black English Usage (N = 88)

Age	n	M	SD
25-41 yrs.	30	1.93	.96
42-56 yrs.	29	1.24	.68
57 yrs. or older	29	1.69	.78
Total	88	1.62	.86

Table 25.

Analysis of Variance for Age by Importance of Constant Correction of Black English Usage (N = 88)

Source	SS	df	MS	F	p
Between groups	7.11	2	3.55	5.32	.01*
Within groups	56.76	85	.67		
Total	63.86	87			

Note. *Significant at the $p < .05$ level

Table 26.

Tukey's HSD for Age by Constant Correction of Black English Usage (N = 88)

Tukey's Multiple Comparisons

(I) Age (banded)	(J) Age (banded)	Mean difference (I - J)	SE	p
25-41 yrs.	42-56 yrs.	.68*	.21	.01*
	57 yrs. and older	.23	.21	.52
42-56 yrs.	25-41 yrs.	-.68*	.21	.01*
	57 yrs. and older	-.45	.22	.10
57 yrs. or older	25-41 yrs.	-.23	.21	.52
	42-56 yrs.	.45	.22	.10

Note. *Significant at the $p < .05$ level

Research question three. Is there a difference between English/language arts teachers' level of education and their perceptions across the three clusters: (a) communicative competence regarding Black English, (b) challenge of teaching Standard English to Black English speakers, and (c) importance of constant correction of Black English usage? The Mann-Whitney U analysis used bachelor's and graduate groups for comparison across each cluster.

The Mann-Whitney U test examined central tendency comparisons of the two *level of education* groups because these groups were non-proportional and violated the normal distribution and homogeneous variance assumptions for the ANOVA. Tables 27-32 show the mean ranks and Mann-Whitney U test results for highest level

64

of education of respondents with regard to each cluster. The Mann-Whitney U analysis showed no statistically significant difference ($z = -.75$, $p = .45$, two-tailed) in the *Communicative Competence Regarding Black English* ranking between the bachelor's ($M_{rank} = 39.82$) and graduate ($M_{rank} = 45.39$) groups. Tables 27-28 show the mean ranks and Mann-Whitney U results for bachelor's and graduate groups with respect to the *Communicative Competence Regarding Black English* cluster.

Table 27.

Mean Ranks for Highest Level of Education by Communicative Competence Regarding Black English (N = 88)

Level of education	n	Mean rank
Bachelor's	14	39.82
Graduate	74	45.39

Table 28.

Mann-Whitney U for Highest Level of Education by Communicative Competence Regarding Black English (N = 88)

Source	Value
Mann-Whitney U	452.50
Wilcoxon W	557.50
z	-.75
Asymmetrical significance (two-tailed)	.45

The Mann-Whitney U analysis depicted no statistically significant difference ($z = -1.00$, $p = .32$, two-tailed) in the *Challenge of Teaching Standard English to Black English Speakers* ranking between the bachelor's ($\underline{M}_{rank} = 50.71$) and graduate ($\underline{M}_{rank} = 43.32$) groups. Tables 29-30 provide the mean ranks and Mann-Whitney U results for bachelor's and graduate groups with respect to the *Challenge of Teaching Standard English to Black English Speakers* cluster.

Table 29.

Mean Ranks for Highest Level of Education by Challenge of Teaching Standard English to Black English Speakers (N = 88)

Level of education	*n*	Mean rank
Bachelor's	14	50.71
Graduate	74	43.32

Table 30.

Mann-Whitney U for Highest Level of Education by Challenge of Teaching Standard English to Black English Speakers (N = 88)

Source	Value
Mann-Whitney U	431.00
Wilcoxon W	3206.00
z	-1.00
Asymmetrical significance (two-tailed)	.32

The Mann-Whitney U analysis displayed no statistically significant difference ($z = -1.42$, $p = .16$, two-tailed) in the *Importance of Constant Correction of Black English Usage* ranking between the bachelor's ($M_{rank} = 53.39$) and graduate ($M_{rank} = 42.82$) groups. Tables 31-32 show the mean ranks and Mann-Whitney U results for bachelor's and graduate groups across the *Importance of Constant Correction of Black English Usage* cluster.

Table 31.

Mean Ranks for Highest Level of Education by Importance of Constant Correction of Black English Usage (N = 88)

Level of education	*n*	Mean rank
Bachelor's	14	53.39
Graduate	74	42.82

Table 32.

Mann-Whitney U for Highest Level of Education by Importance of Constant Correction of Black English Usage (N = 88)

Source	Value
Mann-Whitney U	393.50
Wilcoxon W	3168.50
z	-1.42
Asymmetrical significance (two-tailed)	.16

Although the Mann-Whitney U results indicated no statistical significance regarding *highest level of education*, certain trends emerged from the data. Bachelor's groups (M_{rank} = 50.71) reflected a higher mean rank than graduate groups (M_{rank} = 53.39) on the cluster, *Challenge of Teaching SE to BE Speakers*. Bachelor's groups (M_{rank} = 53.39) also showed a higher mean rank than graduate groups (M_{rank} = 42.82) on the *Importance of Constant Correction of Black English Usage* cluster. These trends suggested that ELA teachers possessing only bachelor's degrees tended to agree at a higher rate than teachers with graduate degrees that teaching Standard English to Black English speakers is a challenging task. In addition, teachers possessing only bachelor's degrees were more likely than teachers with graduate degrees to favor constant correction of Black English usage.

Research question four. Is there a difference between English/language arts teachers' gender and their perceptions across the three clusters: (a) communicative competence regarding Black English, (b) challenge of teaching Standard English to Black English speakers, and (c) importance of constant correction of Black English usage? The Mann-Whitney U test examined central tendency comparisons of the two gender groups because these groups were non-proportional and violated the normal distribution and homogeneous variance assumptions for the ANOVA. Tables 33-38 provide the mean ranks and Mann-Whitney U results for gender across each cluster.

The Mann-Whitney U analysis showed no statistically significant difference (z = -.67, p = .50, two-tailed) in the *Communicative Competence Regarding Black English* ranking between the female (M_{rank} = 45.39) and male (M_{rank} = 40.76) groups. Tables 33-34 show the mean ranks and Mann-Whitney U results for female and male respondents for the *Communicative Competence Regarding Black English* cluster.

Table 33.

Mean Ranks for Gender by Communicative Competence Regarding Black English (N = 88)

Gender	n	Mean rank
Female	71	45.39
Male	17	40.76

Table 34.

Mann-Whitney U for Gender by Communicative Competence Regarding Black English (N = 88)

Source	Value
Mann-Whitney U	540.00
Wilcoxon W	693.00
z	-.67
Asymmetrical significance (two-tailed)	.50

The Mann-Whitney U analysis revealed a statistically significant difference (z = -2.21, p < .05, two-tailed) in the *Challenge of Teaching Standard English to Black English Speakers* ranking between the female ($\underline{M}_{rank}$ = 41.58) and male ($\underline{M}_{rank}$ = 56.71) groups. Tables 35-36 provide the mean ranks and Mann-Whitney U results for female and male respondents relative to the *Challenge of Teaching Standard English to Black English Speakers* cluster.

Table 35.

Mean Ranks for Gender by Challenge of Teaching Standard English to Black English Speakers (N = 88)

Gender	n	Mean rank
Female	71	41.58
Male	17	56.71

Table 36.

Mann-Whitney U for Gender by Challenge of Teaching Standard English to Black English Speakers (N = 88)

Source	Value
Mann-Whitney U	396.00
Wilcoxon W	2952.00
z	-2.21
Asymmetrical significance (two-tailed)	.03*

Note. *Significant at the $p < .05$ level

    The Mann-Whitney U analysis indicated no statistically significant difference ($z = -.18$, two-tailed $p = .86$) in the *Importance of Constant Correction of Black English Usage* ranking between the female ($\underline{M}_{rank} = 44.26$) and male ($\underline{M}_{rank} = 45.50$) groups. Tables 37-38 show the mean ranks and Mann-Whitney U results for female and male respondents with respect to the *Importance of Constant Correction of Black English Usage* cluster.

Table 37.

Mean Ranks for Gender by Importance of Constant Correction of Black English Usage (N = 88)

Gender	*n*	Mean rank
Female	71	44.26
Male	17	45.50

Table 38.

Mann-Whitney U for Gender by Importance of Constant Correction of Black English Usage (N = 88)

Source	Value
Mann-Whitney U	586.50
Wilcoxon W	3142.50
z	-.18
Asymmetrical significance (two-tailed)	.86

Results from the Mann-Whitney U revealed statistical significance within the *Challenge of Teaching Standard English to Black English Speakers* cluster. This finding suggested that male (M_{rank} = 56.71) teachers were more likely than female (M_{rank}= 41.58) teachers to agree that teaching Standard English to Black English speakers is a challenging task. The mean rank differences in the *Importance of Constant Correction of Black English Usage* cluster were not significant. However, the Mann-Whitney U results suggested that the male respondents (M_{rank} = 45.50) rated the *Importance of Constant*

Correction of Black English Usage cluster higher than females ($\underline{M}$ rank = 44.26). This finding suggested that males were more likely than females to favor constant correction of Black English usage.

Research question five. Is there a difference between English/language arts teachers' years of experience as an educator and their perceptions across the three clusters: (a) communicative competence regarding Black English, (b) challenge of teaching Standard English to Black English speakers, and (c) importance of constant correction of Black English usage? One-way analysis of variance (ANOVA) tested the difference in sample means for participants' years of experience as an educator.

Results from the ANOVA analysis showed no statistical significance in the sample means for years of experience as an educator on the cluster, *Communicative Competence Regarding Black English,* $F(2, 87) = 1.30$, $p = .26$. Tables 39-40 display the means, standard deviations, and ANOVA results for teacher's years of experience as an educator across the *Communicative Competence Regarding Black English* cluster.

Table 39.

Means and Standard Deviations for Years of Experience as an Educator by Communicative Competence Regarding Black English (N = 88)

Years of experience	*n*	*M*	*SD*
1-15 yrs.	39	2.68	.80
16+ yrs.	49	2.87	.80
Total	88	2.79	.80

Table 40.

Analysis of Variance for Years of Experience as an Educator by
Communicative Competence Regarding Black English (N = 88)

Source	SS	df	MS	F	p
Between groups	.82	1	.82	1.30	.26
Within groups	54.32	86	.63		
Total	55.14	87			

Results from the ANOVA analysis exhibited no statistical significance in the sample means for years of experience as an educator on the cluster, *Challenge of Teaching Standard English to Black English Speakers*, $F(1, 87) = 1.56$, $p = .21$. Tables 41-42 show the means, standard deviations, and ANOVA results for teacher's years of experience as an educator across the *Challenge of Teaching Standard English to Black English Speakers* cluster.

Table 41.

Means and Standard Deviations for Years of Experience as an
Educator by Challenge of Teaching SE to BE Speakers (N = 88)

Years of experience	n	M	SD
1-15 yrs.	39	2.02	.77
16+ yrs.	49	1.82	.76
Total	88	1.91	.77

Table 42.

Analysis of Variance for Years of Experience as an Educator by Challenge of Teaching Standard English to Black English Speakers (N = 88)

Source	SS	df	MS	F	p
Between groups	.91	1	.91	1.56	.21
Within groups	50.19	86	.58		
Total	51.10	87			

Results from the ANOVA analysis showed no statistical significance in the sample means for years of experience as an educator on the cluster, *Importance of Constant Correction of Black English Usage*, $F(1, 87) = 1.60$, $p = .21$. Tables 43-44 show the means, standard deviations, and ANOVA results for teacher's years of experience as an educator across the *Importance of Constant Correction of Black English Usage* cluster.

Table 43.

Means and Standard Deviations for Years of Experience as an Educator by Importance of Constant Correction of Black English Usage (N = 88)

Years of experience	n	M	SD
1-15 yrs.	39	1.75	.95
16+ yrs.	49	1.52	.77
Total	88	1.62	.86

Table 44.

Analysis of Variance for Years of Experience as an Educator by
Importance of Constant Correction of Black English Usage (N = 88)

Source	SS	df	MS	F	p
Between groups	1.17	1	1.17	1.60	21
Within groups	62.70	86	.73		
Total	63.86	87			

Although the one-way ANOVA results indicated no statistically significant difference in respondents' means for the *years of experience as an educator* variable, specific trends emerged from the data. ELA teachers with 1-15 years of experience had a higher mean (*M* = 2.02) than ELA teachers with 16 or more years of experience (*M* = 1.82) on the *Challenge of Teaching Standard English to Black English Speakers* cluster. This finding suggested that ELA teachers with least experience were more apt to agree that teaching Standard English to Black English speakers is a challenging task. ELA teachers with 1-15 years of experience also had a higher mean (*M* = 1.75) than ELA teachers with 16 or more years of experience (*M* = 1.52) on the *Importance of Constant Correction of Black English Usage* cluster. This finding suggested that ELA teachers with least experience were more inclined to favor constant correction of Black English usage.

Research question six. Is there a difference between English/language arts teachers' academic training in non-standard English dialects and their perceptions across the three clusters: (a) communicative competence regarding Black English, (b) challenge of teaching Standard English to Black English speakers, and (c) importance of constant correction of Black English usage? One-way analysis of variance (ANOVA) tested the difference in sample means for academic training in nonstandard English dialects. Tables 45-50 show the means, standard deviations, and ANOVA results for academic training in nonstandard English dialects with respect to each cluster.

Results from the ANOVA analysis displayed no statistical significance in the sample means for teachers' academic training in nonstandard English dialects on the cluster, *Communicative Competence Regarding Black English*, $F(1, 87) = .14$, $p = .71$. Tables 45-46 provide the means, standard deviations, and ANOVA results for teachers' academic training in nonstandard English dialects on the *Communicative Competence Regarding Black English* cluster.

Table 45.

Means and Standard Deviations for Academic Training in Nonstandard English Dialects by Communicative Competence Regarding BE (N = 88)

Academic training	*n*	*M*	*SD*
Some training	36	2.83	.89
No training	52	2.76	.73
Total	88	2.79	.80

Table 46.

Analysis of Variance for Academic Training in Nonstandard English Dialects by Communicative Competence Regarding BE Usage (N = 88)

Source	*SS*	*df*	*MS*	*F*	*p*
Between groups	.09	1	.09	.14	.71
Within groups	55.05	86	.64		
Total	55.14	87			

Results from the ANOVA analysis exhibited no statistical significance in the sample means for teachers' academic training in nonstandard English dialects on the cluster, *Challenge of Teaching Standard English to Black English Speakers*, $F(1, 87) = .88$, $p = .35$. Tables 47-48 display the means, standard deviations, and ANOVA results for teachers' academic training in non-standard English dialects relative to the *Challenge of Teaching Standard English to Black English Speakers* cluster.

Table 47.

Means and Standard Deviations for Academic Training in Nonstandard English Dialects by Challenge of Teaching SE to BE Speakers (N = 88)

Academic training	n	M	SD
Some training	36	1.81	.80
No training	52	1.97	.74
Total	88	1.91	.77

Table 48.

Analysis of Variance for Academic Training in Nonstandard English Dialects by Challenge of Teaching SE to BE Speakers (N = 88)

Source	SS	df	MS	F	p
Between groups	.52	1	.52	.88	.35
Within groups	50.58	86	.59		
Total	51.10	87			

Results from the ANOVA analysis presented no statistical significance in the sample means for teachers' academic training in nonstandard English dialects on the cluster, *Importance of Constant Correction of Black English Usage*, $F(1, 87) = .94, p = .34$. Tables 49-50 show the means, standard deviations, and ANOVA results for teachers' academic training in nonstandard English dialects relative to the *Importance of Constant Correction of Black English Usage* cluster.

Table 49.

Means and Standard Deviations for Academic Training in Nonstandard English Dialects by Importance of Constant Correction of BE Usage (N = 88)

Academic training	n	M	SD
Some training	36	1.73	.83
No training	52	1.55	.88
Total	88	1.62	.86

Table 50.

Analysis of Variance for Academic Training in Nonstandard English Dialects by Importance of Constant Correction of BE Usage (N = 88)

Source	SS	df	MS	F	p
Between groups	.69	1	.69	.94	.34
Within groups	63.17	86	.74		
Total	63.86	87			

Although the one-way ANOVA results showed no statistically significant differences in respondents' means for the *academic training in nonstandard English dialects* variable, trends emerged from the data. English/language arts teachers with academic training in nonstandard English dialects ($M = 2.83$) had a higher mean than ELA teachers with no academic training ($M = 2.76$) on the *Communicative Competence Regarding Black English* cluster. This finding suggested that ELA teachers who had been trained in nonstandard English dialects were more inclined to agree that they possessed communicative competence with regard to communicating with Black English speakers.

ELA teachers with academic training in nonstandard English dialects and ELA teachers with no academic training tended to disagree with constant correction of Black English usage. However, ELA teachers with training ($M = 1.73$) rated the *Constant Correction of Black English Usage* cluster higher than ELA teachers with no training ($M = 1.55$). This result suggested that ELA teachers who had been trained in nonstandard English dialects were slightly more likely than ELA teachers with no training to favor constant correction of Black English usage.

Research question seven. Is there a difference between grade level(s) taught and English/language arts teachers' perceptions across the three clusters: (a) communicative competence regarding Black English, (b) challenge of teaching Standard English to Black English speakers, and (c) importance of constant correction of Black English usage? The Mann-Whitney U analysis showed no statistically significant difference ($z = -.63$, $p = .53$, two-tailed) in the *Communicative Competence Regarding Black English* ranking between the *one level taught* ($\underline{M}_{rank} = 43.82$) and *two or more levels taught* ($\underline{M}_{rank} = 48.79$) groups. Tables 51-52 show the mean ranks and Mann-Whitney U results for *one level taught* and *two or more levels taught* groups with respect to the *Communicative Competence Regarding Black English* cluster.

Table 51.

Mean Ranks for Grade Level(s) Taught by Communicative Competence Regarding Black English (N = 88)

Grade level (s) taught	n	Mean rank
One level	76	43.82
Two or more levels	12	48.79

Table 52.

Mann-Whitney U for Grade Level(s) Taught by Communicative Competence Regarding Black English (N = 88)

Source	Value
Mann-Whitney U	404.50
Wilcoxon W	3330.50
z	-.63
Asymmetrical significance (two-tailed)	.53

The Mann-Whitney U analysis showed no statistically significant difference ($z = -.15$, $p = .88$, two-tailed) in the *Challenge of Teaching Standard English to Black English Speakers* ranking between the *one level taught* ($\underline{M}_{rank} = 44.66$) and *two or more levels taught* ($\underline{M}_{rank} = 43.46$) groups. Tables 53-54 provide the mean ranks and Mann-Whitney U results for *one level taught* and *two or more levels taught* groups across the *Challenge of Teaching Standard English to Black English Speakers* cluster.

Table 53.

Mean Ranks for Grade Level(s) Taught by Challenge of Teaching Standard English to Black English Speakers (N = 88)

Grade level(s) taught	n	Mean rank
One level	76	44.66
Two or more levels	12	43.46

Table 54.

Mann-Whitney U for Grade Level(s) Taught by Challenge of Teaching Standard English to Black English Speakers (N = 88)

Source	Value
Mann-Whitney U	443.50
Wilcoxon W	521.50
z	-.15
Asymmetrical significance (two-tailed)	.88

The Mann-Whitney U analysis indicated no statistically significant difference (z = -1.80, p = .07, two-tailed) in the *Importance of Constant Correction of Black English Usage* ranking between the *one level* (M_{rank} = 46.44) and *two or more levels* (M_{rank} = 32.21) groups. Tables 55-56 show the mean ranks and Mann-Whitney U results for ELA teachers who taught only one grade level and ELA teachers who taught two or more grade levels across the *Importance of Constant Correction of Black English Usage* cluster.

Table 55.

Mean Ranks for Grade Level(s) Taught by Importance of Constant Correction of Black English Usage (N = 88)

Grade level(s) taught	n	Mean rank
One level	76	46.44
Two or more levels	12	32.21

Table 56.

Mann-Whitney U for Grade Level(s) Taught by Importance of Constant Correction of Black English Usage (N = 88)

Source	Value
Mann-Whitney U	308.50
Wilcoxon W	386.50
z	-1.80
Asymmetrical significance (two-tailed)	.07

The Mann-Whitney U results reflected no statistically significant differences in mean ranks on the *grade level(s) taught* variable. However, certain trends emerged from the data. English/language arts teachers who taught only one grade level (M_{rank} = 43.82) rated the *Communicative Competence Regarding Black English* cluster lower than ELA teachers who taught two or more grade levels (M_{rank} = 48.79). However, ELA teachers who taught only one grade level (M_{rank} = 44.66) rated the *Challenge of Teaching Standard English to Black English Speakers* cluster higher than ELA teachers who taught two or more grade levels (M_{rank} = 43.46). The findings for the *Importance of Constant Correction of Black English Usage* cluster also showed that ELA teachers who taught only one grade level (M_{rank} = 46.44) rated this cluster higher than ELA teachers who taught two or more grade levels (M_{rank} = 32.21).

These trends suggested that ELA teachers who taught only one level (elementary or secondary vs. elementary and secondary) were less likely to agree that they possessed communicative competence when communicating with Black English speakers. These teachers were also more likely to favor constant correction of Black English usage and agree that teaching Standard English to Black English speakers is a challenging task.

Fixed-response and Qualitative Data Analyses

Four additional research questions examined ELA teachers' perceptions of Black English, which included a fixed-response question and three qualitative questions. Respectively, these questions focused on ELA teachers' perceptions regarding: (a) the frequency of specific BE features evidenced in BE speakers' writing, (b) concerns when teaching Standard English to Black English speakers, (c) recommendations for professional development, and (d) useful advice for beginning teachers of Black English speakers. The researcher analyzed all responses to open-ended questions. Through the use of content analysis measures such as codification and categorization, the researcher identified major themes that emerged from the data.

Research question eight. What do English/language arts teachers perceive to be the three most frequent Black English features evidenced in BE-speaking students' writing? For item #23 of the survey questionnaire, the researcher provided eleven examples of common Black English features. As indicated on the questionnaire, items 23a-23k included examples of: (a) copula absence, (b) habitual *be*, (c) aspectual *BEEN*, (d) consonant-cluster reduction (e.g., omission of *–ed*), (e) substitution of /k/ for /t/; (f) subject-verb disagreement (e.g., The boy *run* quickly); (g) absence of possessive *–s* (e.g., My *teacher* pencil broke), (h) aspectual DONE (e.g., He *done* finished his homework), (i) voiced /th/ substituted for /d/ (e.g., they vs. *dey*), (j) voiceless /th/ substituted for /f/ or /v/ (e.g., bath vs. *baf*), and (k) negative concord (e.g., *Nobody don't want none*).

In order to analyze participants' responses on this particular survey item, the researcher employed SPSS 12.0, using frequencies and percentages to calculate responses. Results from the frequency tables revealed three most frequent BE features evidenced in BE-speaking students' writing. According to the data, most sample participants selected survey items 23a, 23b, and 23f, depicting *habitual be, copula absence,* and *subject-verb disagreement* as the three Black English features most frequently evidenced in BE-speaking students' writing.

Habitual *be* involves BE speakers' use of the word *be* to substitute occasions where Standard English speakers use adverbs such as *sometimes* or *usually* (e.g., She *be* here vs. She *is usually* here). Copula absence occurs when BE speakers fail to employ "to be" verbs such as *is* and *are* in oral or written expression. In lieu of writing, "She is here," a BE speaker may write, "She here," thus omitting the copula, or "to be" verb. As indicated in Table 57, habitual *be* received the highest percentage (52.3%), followed by subject-verb disagreement (45.5%) and copula absence (43.2%).

Table 57.

Black English Features Most Frequently Evidenced in Students'
Writing (N = 88)

Variable	Frequency	Percent
Habitual *be*	46	52.3
Subject-verb disagreement	40	45.5
Copula absence	38	43.2

Note. Actual N = 88. The allowance of multiple responses resulted in more than 100% frequency.

Research question nine. What concerns do English language arts teachers have with regard to teaching BE-speaking students to speak or write in Standard English? Survey participants offered specific comments relating to their concerns about teaching Standard English to BE-speaking students. Three major themes emerged from the data.

The most cited concern involved the need for Black English speakers to recognize the relevance of having a sense of audience and purpose in spoken and written discourse in order to become successful in mainstream society. One teacher/ participant expressed, "I tried to impress upon all my students the need for a sense of audience . . . Correct use of Standard English is necessary in college applications, job interviews, conversations." Another respondent noted, "A concern I have is that BE-speaking students are not given equal consideration and training as to when to shift language register for purpose and audience." A different participant wrote:

I stress the importance of considering the audience
when speaking and writing. I encourage my
BE-speaking students to speak in the best way to
communicate with a particular audience. With friends
at the mall-speak informally. At a job interview-
speak formally. They need to understand that language
is a tool that we manipulate for specific purposes.

One teacher wrote, "My concern is for their success, or lack of success, in the workforce due to BE-speaking." Other responses included concerns with BE-speaking students being "expected to have control of Standard English" and having "code-switching" abilities, or being "able to move comfortably back and forth between BE and standard English."

A second concern that surfaced was ELA teachers' frustration resulting from BE-speakers' inability to recognize the need for Standard English instruction. One respondent noted that the BE-speakers "don't understand why it matters." Some teachers revealed the frustration that results from trying to persuade BE speakers to use Standard English. One participant explained that "as a white teacher, it is difficult to persuade BE students to use standard English in formal writing/settings w/out offending/disrespecting their culture."

Another teacher emphasized that ". . . students who speak BE often write the way they talk. This frustrates me at times because when we go over or review their writing, they can often pick out their mistakes, but not until they re-read it several times." Other respondents were concerned with the idea that "they speak it at home and with friends so they feel it is acceptable everywhere." One teacher summarized this concern:

Orally, outside the classroom, its use continues to be
reinforced in their home and peer groups. I try to
emphasize that the written aspect of language must
be 'standard' and that they should work hard on the
oral use of language as well, since many first
impressions are made from someone's speech.
It is frustrating . . .

ELA teachers expressed the need to find a balance between enforcing Standard English and being culturally responsive to diverse learners. One participant noted that a "concern when teaching BE-speaking students, or other ESL students, is how to find the balance between their own spoken language and standard English." Another teacher asked, "How do I respect culture and still teach students to write for a more traditional audience?" A different respondent posed a similar question, "How do you correct them without infringing on cultural norms?" Other participants were concerned with "accusations of racism" and "crossing the fine line between encouraging students to be able to work and communicate with all people and implying that their learned language pattern is inferior, which I don't feel it is."

Research question ten. What professional development would English/language arts teachers find helpful for teaching BE-speaking students Standard English? Sample participants recommended various types of professional development they felt would be helpful when teaching Standard English to Black English speakers. Based on the majority of the responses, two dominant recommendations emerged from the data.

The most common recommendation involved ELA teachers' perceived need for training in the structure of Black English dialect in order to develop *contrastive analysis* and *code-switching* skills for comparative instruction. As defined in research literature, the contrastive analysis technique involves identifying similarities and differences between Black English and Standard English. Code-switching involves opportunities in which people learn to alter their speech and behavioral patterns to conform to certain situations. They are able to make smooth transitions from one language or dialect to another (Celious & Oyserman, 2001; Dandy, 1991; Smitherman, 2000). One respondent asked, "Are there BE texts that could be used for comparative instruction?" Additional responses from participants that supported this finding included:

- "Appropriate ways to coach students regarding when to choose BE or SE. Instruction for teachers to know and understand BE as a distinct dialect."

- ". . . creating flexible curriculum that has both components would be a useful focus for professional development."

- "Strategies on ways to incorporate BE in the classroom, to cross over between BE [to] SE or SE [to] BE, and when/how/why/ to correct."

- "Methods to help students internalize the differences and uses of SE vs. BE, and to know when it is appropriate to use each dialect."

- "Not so much what constitutes BE but perhaps grammatical structures that we can use as 'parallels' when teaching standard English. I imagine some of the same principles that foreign language teachers use to teach a new language."

- "To first understand Black English myself, so that I can know when it is appropriate to use each dialect."

- "Workshops to help students decide when [BE] is important.

- "Strategies focusing on <u>transition</u> from BE to Standard English (ex., addressing how to go from "he <u>be</u> walking to he <u>is</u> walking."

The latter statement revealed one ELA teacher's incorrect comparison of the habitual *be* in Black English with the "to be" verb in Standard English. This finding further supported the perceived need for ELA teachers to become more familiar with Black English dialect.

Another common professional development recommendation addressed the concern of finding a balance between teaching Standard English while maintaining cultural sensitivity. Some participants recommended professional development training focused on ways to achieve this balance through "research" and "awareness sessions." One respondent desired assistance on "ways to help [BE speakers] understand how to use SE without offending them." Another participant wrote, "I have taken classes (undergraduate and graduate) about language theory, acquisition and writing. What I feel is missing in my relationships w/non-white students is an in-depth understanding of their culture, which would help me find the balance of when to insist on standard English." Other participants indicated a desire for "a sociolinguistic course in [Black English]" and "trainings—seminars— through the intermediate units, etc." in order to be able to "recognize cultural differences."

Research question eleven. What advice would English language arts teachers give beginning teachers in regard to teaching Standard English to BE-speaking students? Survey participants offered several suggestions for beginning teachers of BE-speaking students. However, two dominant themes emerged. First, teachers expressed the need to remain patient and culturally sensitive when teaching Standard English to BE-speaking students. One participant suggested that teachers "be patient!—Model, don't preach, SE." A different teacher noted that beginning teachers should "be gentle and understand [Black English] is part of their culture!" Another respondent advised beginning teachers to:

> Be patient when teaching skills; know your students;
> Never embarrass anyone; Read many African American
> authors; Use examples of many cultures that have
> influenced SE; Celebrate diversity in your classroom;
> Listen—you'll learn many beautiful things—let your
> students teach you . . .

Other responses included the need for beginning teachers to "not become confrontational or condescending," "treat all students with respect and value each student," and "clearly identify when informal language (BE) is appropriate and when SE is necessary."

A second theme that emerged from the data was for beginning teachers to emphasize Standard English while valuing students and avoiding excessive corrective measures. Recommendations suggested that beginning teachers realize that "it's important to not go overboard with correction." One person noted, "Go slow. Don't attack the student or the dialect." Another participant wrote, "Drill and kill is inappropriate. Students can't and won't make the transfer on their own to SE. Teachers must find ways to integrate SE instruction into a classroom that encourages communication by all students however they speak/write." Other participants advised beginning teachers to "use focus correction areas instead of overwhelming students w/everything at once" and to "value and learn from them." A final participant explained that ". . . if kids know you care, they will try to accomplish nearly any task to make the teacher proud."

Summary of Major Findings

Using descriptive, inferential, and content analysis methods for the study, the researcher discovered pertinent findings based on survey participants' responses. The following report of major research findings is prefaced, however, with the need to reveal that results may be subject to bias given the characteristics of this sample population and low response rate. (See Appendix B for supplements to the study.)

Respondents' Demographical Data

The demographic variables for the study included ethnicity, highest level of education, gender, years of experience as an educator, academic training in nonstandard English dialects, age, and grade level(s) taught. The sample population consisted of 88.6% White and 11.4% non-White ELA teachers. Of this sample, 80.7% of the respondents were female and 19.3% were male.

With respect to highest level of education, 15.9% of the population obtained only bachelor's degrees, whereas 84.1% earned graduate degrees. Regarding years of experience as an educator, 55.7% of the respondents had 16 or more years of experience, whereas 44.3% had 1-15 years of experience. In addition, 40.9% of the sample indicated that they were trained in nonstandard English dialects, but 59.1% had not received any training in this area. Respondents' ages ranged from 25 to 70 years. As a categorical variable, the age percentages were almost equal: 25-41 years (34.1%), 42-56 years (33.0%), and 57 years or older (33.0%). Finally, data indicated that 86.4% of the respondents taught only one grade level (elementary or secondary), whereas 13.6% of the participants taught two or more grade levels (elementary and secondary). Although the demographical data among research participants varied, data revealed that the majority of the sample comprised middle-aged, White women. The higher percentage of White teachers reaffirmed findings regarding the shortage of minority teachers in the public school system (Spring, 2002). In addition, the majority of these teachers earned graduate degrees and had approximately two decades of teaching experience. Results showed that these teachers lacked training in nonstandard English dialects, which supported the assertion of linguists and other scholars concerning the dearth of linguistic training among teachers (Baugh, 2000; Matsuda, 2006; Smitherman, 2000).

Findings for Survey Items and Research Questions

Survey item and cluster analyses revealed that approximately 70% of the respondents tended to agree that they were able to communicate well with BE-speaking students. Approximately 70% of the participants tended to disagree with constant correction of BE usage. These findings suggested that the majority of ELA teachers in the sample believed they were able to communicate adequately with Black English speakers and that constant correction was not appropriate when teaching BE speakers during language arts instruction.

Research question one. Is there a difference between English/ language arts teachers' ethnicity and their perceptions across the three clusters: (a) communicative competence regarding Black English, (b) challenge of teaching Standard English to Black English speakers, and (c) importance of constant correction of Black English usage? Inferential statistics showed no statistical significance regarding ethnicity. However, results from the mean ranks showed trends in the data pertaining to ethnicity.

Non-White English/language arts teachers (M_{rank} = 52.65) were more likely than White ELA teachers (M_{rank} = 43.46) to agree they possessed communicative competence when communicating with Black English speakers. As operationally defined, communicative competence refers to the ability to produce socially acceptable utterances which would normally be part of a native speaker's competence in a particular language (Hymes, 1974). Coelho (2004) referred to communicative

91

competence as the ability to effectively communicate in real situations. This finding implied that minority teachers felt more confident in their ability to communicate with Black English speakers, whereas White teachers felt less confident. This finding may result from the notion that some non-White teachers are more familiar with nonstandard dialects because some of them may be bidialectal (i.e., able to understand/speak both nonstandard and Standard English).

Non-White respondents ($M_{rank} = 54.20$) were more favorable toward constant correction of Black English usage than White respondents ($M_{rank} = 43.26$). This result suggested that, because of their minority status, non-White respondents may be more apt to recognize the social stigma inherent in BE usage and the societal privileges associated with Standard English (Craig & Washington, 2002; Delpit, 1995; Smitherman, 2000). For example, one non-White participant wrote, "Teach students to love reading and writing first. Then, correct them (show them the value of correcting writing/speaking); speak openly about BE. Don't ignore that it exists."

This finding suggested that some White teachers may feel uneasy about correcting BE speakers, fearing that BE speakers will become offended by constant correction. Participants' written comments further supported this assumption, relating to concerns such as "accusations of racism" and that "as a white teacher, it is difficult to persuade BE students to use standard English . . . without offending/ disrespecting their culture." Another respondent wrote:

> Many of my Black students are insulted when
> corrected. They tell me that it is 'White' to speak/
> write in standard English. Many or most of the
> Black students refuse to make corrections on
> written work. I have good rapport with these
> students; I just don't know how to get past this
> barrier.

These findings supported the sample participants' perceived need for professional development opportunities directed toward increased cultural awareness.

Research question two. Is there a difference between English/ language arts teachers' age and their perceptions across the three clusters: (a) communicative competence regarding Black English, (b) challenge of teaching Standard English to Black English speakers, and (c) importance of constant correction of Black English usage? The ANOVA analysis revealed statistical significance within the cluster, *Importance of Constant Correction of Black English Usage*, $F(2, 88) =$ 5.32, $p < .05$. Results from Tukey's HSD test indicated that statistically significant differences were between 25-41 year-olds and 42-56 year-olds at the $p < .05$ level.

These findings suggested that all age groups tended to disagree with respect to the *Constant Correction of Black English Usage* cluster. However, 25-41 year-olds ($M = 1.93$) were more inclined to favor constant correction of Black English usage than respondents who were 42-56 years old ($M = 1.24$) and 57 years old or older ($M = 1.69$). This result suggested that the interconnectedness of youth and nominal training may assume greater tendencies for constant correction.

Research question three. Is there a difference between English/ language arts teachers' level of education and their perceptions across the three clusters: (a) communicative competence regarding Black English, (b) challenge of teaching Standard English to Black English speakers, and (c) importance of constant correction of Black English usage? The Mann-Whitney U results showed no statistical significance regarding highest level of education. However, the data reflected pertinent trends.

ELA teachers with only bachelor's degrees ($M_{rank} = 50.71$) were more likely than teachers with graduate degrees ($M_{rank} = 43.32$) to agree that teaching Standard English to Black English speakers is a challenging task. This finding implied that the amount of education a teacher receives is directly related to their perceptions regarding their ability to teach Standard English language learners. ELA teachers with graduate degrees seemed to feel more confident toward their ability to successfully teach Standard English to Black English speakers.

Teachers with only bachelor's degrees ($M_{rank} = 53.39$) were more likely than teachers with graduate degrees ($M_{rank} = 42.82$) to favor constant correction of Black English usage. This result suggested that ELA teachers who obtained higher education were more reluctant to constantly correct students, possibly recognizing the risk of detrimental effects on student performance. Some survey respondents' comments supported this finding when referring to the need to "correct with diplomacy," and not go "overboard with correction."

Research question four. Is there a difference between English/ language arts teachers' gender and their perceptions across the three clusters: (a) communicative competence regarding Black English, (b) challenge of teaching Standard English to Black English speakers, and (c) importance of constant correction of Black English usage? Results from the Mann-Whitney U revealed statistical significance within the *Challenge of Teaching Standard English to Black English Speakers* cluster. Male ($\underline{M}$ $_{rank}$ = 56.71) respondents ranked the *Challenge of Teaching Standard English to Black English Speakers* cluster higher than female respondents ($\underline{M}$ $_{rank}$ = 41.58). This finding suggested that male ELA teachers felt more uncertain than female teachers about how to effectively teach Standard English to Black English speakers.

The mean rank differences in the *Importance of Constant Correction of Black English Usage* cluster were not significant. However, the Mann-Whitney U results showed that male respondents ($\underline{M}$ $_{rank}$ = 45.50) rated the *Importance of Constant Correction of Black English Usage* cluster higher than females ($\underline{M}$ $_{rank}$ = 44.26). This finding suggested that males were more inclined than females to constantly correct Black English usage. This result may imply that the tendency of male teachers to favor constant correction of Black English usage is associated with their perception that teaching Standard English to BE speakers is a challenging task.

Research question five. Is there a difference between English/ language arts teachers' years of experience as an educator and their perceptions across the three clusters: (a) communicative competence regarding Black English, (b) challenge of teaching Standard English to Black English speakers, and (c) importance of constant correction of Black English usage? The one-way ANOVA results revealed no statistically significant differences in respondents' means relative to their years of experience as an educator. However, the researcher identified trends in the data.

ELA teachers with 1-15 years of experience (M = 2.02) ranked the *Challenge of Teaching Standard English to Black English Speakers* cluster higher than ELA teachers with 16 or more years of experience (M = 1.82). This result suggested that ELA teachers with less experience were more likely than veteran teachers to agree that teaching Standard English to Black English speakers is a challenging task.

Most of the respondents were White (88.6%) and had no training in nonstandard English dialects (59.1%); therefore, it may be safe to assume that most of the less experienced teachers were also White and untrained in this area. These results suggested that White ELA teachers with minimal teaching experience may encounter more challenges not only because of their limited experience but also because of communication barriers resulting from limited knowledge of BE dialect. Limited experience coupled with insufficient training in nonstandard English dialects may further explain why ELA teachers with 1-15 years of experience (M = 1.75) were more inclined than ELA teachers with 16 or more years of experience (M = 1.52) to favor constant correction of Black English usage. Less experienced ELA teachers may have a greater tendency to constantly correct BE usage as a result of an inability to correctly decipher between dialect differences and language deficits (Baugh, 2000; Bland-Stewart, 2005).

Research question six. Is there a difference between English/language arts teachers' academic training in non-standard English dialects and their perceptions across the three clusters: (a) communicative competence regarding Black English, (b) challenge of teaching Standard English to Black English speakers, and (c) importance of constant correction of Black English usage? One-way ANOVA results depicted no statistically significant differences in respondents' means according to participants' academic training in nonstandard English dialects. However, important trends emerged from the data.

ELA teachers who had been trained in nonstandard English dialects (M = 2.83) were more inclined than teachers with no training (M = 2.76) to agree that they possessed communicative competence with regard to communicating with Black English speakers. This finding implied that teachers with training in nonstandard dialects were able to communicate more effectively with nonstandard English speakers than teachers who were not trained.

ELA teachers with academic training in nonstandard English dialects ($M = 1.73$) and those with no academic training in nonstandard English dialects ($M = 1.55$) tended to disagree with constant correction of Black English usage. However, the mean results showed that ELA teachers who had been trained in nonstandard English dialects were somewhat more likely to constantly correct Black English usage. This finding suggested that, although these teachers may have been trained in nonstandard English dialects, they may not have received adequate training specifically in Black English dialect. This lack of training possibly resulted in misunderstandings involving dialect miscues and Standard English errors. Participants' written comments corroborated this assumption when referring to their perceived need for professional development training in Black English dialect.

Research question seven. Is there a difference between English/ language arts teachers' grade level(s) taught and their perceptions across the three clusters: (a) communicative competence regarding Black English, (b) challenge of teaching Standard English to Black English speakers, and (c) importance of constant correction of Black English usage? Mann-Whitney U results showed no statistical significance regarding grade level(s) taught. However, the data revealed interesting trends.

ELA teachers whose teaching experience involved only one grade level (elementary or secondary) ($M_{rank} = 44.66$) were more likely than ELA teachers who taught two or more grade levels ($M_{rank} = 43.46$) to agree that teaching Standard English to Black English speakers is a challenging task. This finding implied that teachers with experience in both elementary and secondary schools may gain a broader perspective on how to teach nonstandard English speakers, thus resulting in greater confidence in their ability to teach this student population. ELA teachers who taught only one grade level ($M_{rank} = 46.44$) were also more likely than ELA teachers who taught two or more (elementary and secondary) grade levels ($M_{rank} = 32.21$) to favor constant correction of Black English usage. Again, this finding suggested that teaching only one grade level may result in a one-sided view of teaching, and therefore, less effective teaching methods.

Research question eight. What do English/language arts teachers perceive to be the three most frequent Black English features evidenced in BE-speaking students' writing? Results from the frequency tables showed that sample participants perceived *habitual be, copula absence,* and *subject-verb disagreement* to be the top three Black English features most frequently evidenced in BE-speaking students' writing. Habitual *be* received the highest percentage, followed by subject-verb disagreement and copula absence.

Although the findings reported three top features, ELA teachers perceived habitual *be* (52.3%) as the feature most frequently evidenced in BE-speaking students' writing. This result supported the claim of LeMoine (2001) and Smitherman (2000) concerning the challenge that mainstream teachers face when teaching BE-speaking students to use mainstream forms of adverbial phrases in lieu of habitual *be*. This result could be explained by the notion that the majority of the teachers in the study were middle-aged, White teachers who lacked linguistic training, and therefore, possessed a limited understanding of how to teach Black English speakers. In addition to focusing on habitual *be,* findings suggested the need for ELA teachers to explore effective means of instructing BE speakers regarding *subject-verb disagreement* and *copula absence* because these features also received high percentages.

Research question nine. What concerns do English/language arts teachers have with regard to teaching BE-speaking students to speak or write in Standard English? Three major themes that emerged from the data included ELA teachers' concerns involving: (a) the need for Black English speakers to recognize the relevance of Standard English instruction, (b) the difficulty White ELA teachers face when teaching BE-speakers to use Standard English, and (c) ELA teachers' perceived need to find a balance between enforcing Standard English and being culturally responsive to diverse learners. These themes shared a commonality of thought, reaffirming the extant communication barrier among some mainstream teachers and Black English speakers (Lemoine, 2001; Smitherman, 2000).

Research question ten. What professional development would English/language arts teachers find helpful for teaching BE-speaking students Standard English? Two major themes surfaced regarding

97

recommendations for professional development. The most prevailing theme involved ELA teachers' perceived need to obtain training in Black English dialect in order to develop contrastive analysis and code-switching skills. This finding suggested that ELA teachers desired to learn more about Black English dialect in order to assist students in identifying similarities and differences between Black English and Standard English. This result supported linguists' assertions regarding the importance of utilizing contrastive analysis and code-switching approaches when teaching Standard English to dialect speakers (Celious & Oyserman, 2001; Dandy, 1991; Green, 2002a; Smitherman, 2000).

Another recommendation for professional development focused on research-based training regarding how ELA teachers may achieve a balance between Standard English enforcement and cultural sensitivity. Teachers revealed a desire to receive "current thinking from the research" on culture and Black English dialect that would enable them to achieve "specific and practical solutions."

Research question eleven. What advice would English/ language arts teachers give beginning teachers in regard to teaching Standard English to BE-speaking students? The majority of the respondents expressed the need for beginning teachers to remain patient and culturally sensitive when teaching Standard English to BE-speaking students. They encouraged beginning teachers to "model, don't preach, SE."

A final recommendation for beginning teachers included the need to value students and correct linguistic differences both gradually and with diplomacy. Respondents emphasized the need for beginning teachers to "understand that changing the way they speak and write will take a lot of time!" Therefore, teachers should take "small steps and build proper grammar constructions with each assignment." These findings supported scholars' assertions that constant correction imposed detrimental effects on English language learners (Coelho, 2004; Delpit, 1995; Snow & Kamhi-Stein, 2006).

Conclusions Based on Findings

The researcher based the following conclusions on findings from the research study:

1. No statistically significant difference exists between English/language arts teachers' ethnicity and their perceptions of Black English usage. This finding suggested that ethnicity does not impact English/ language arts teachers' perceptions toward teaching BE-speaking students. However, this finding may be biased because of the limited number of non-White survey participants.

2. A statistically significant difference exists between English/language arts teachers' age and their perceptions regarding constant correction of Black English usage. This finding suggested that younger teachers may correct Black English speakers at higher rates than older teachers, which could be explained by the notion that novice teachers lack the expertise of more seasoned teachers (Darling-Hammond, 2000).

3. No statistically significant difference exists between English/language arts teachers' level of education and their perceptions of Black English usage. This finding implied that level of education does not impact ELA teachers' perceptions of Black English usage. The finding may have resulted from the older participants' lack of exposure to multicultural education, which did not appear in higher education programs until the 1970s and 1980s (Ibarra, 2006). During this time, some participants presumably received only introductory instruction in multicultural education, whereas others may have already graduated, thus failing to receive any multicultural education.

99

4. A statistically significant difference exists between English/language arts teachers' gender and their perceptions regarding the challenge of teaching Standard English to Black English speakers. Findings showed that male ELA teachers were more likely than female teachers to agree that teaching Standard English to Black English speakers is challenging. This finding may contain bias because few male teachers participated in the study.

5. No statistical significance exists between English/language arts teachers' years of experience and their perceptions of Black English usage. This finding suggested that years of experience does not impact English/language arts teachers' perceptions of BE usage. This result may contain bias because the majority of the participants were White, veteran teachers with 16 or more years of experience as an educator.

6. No statistical significance exists between English/language arts teachers' academic training and their perceptions of Black English usage. This finding may be explained by the notion that over 50% of the respondents had not received training in nonstandard English dialects, possibly because of the lack of linguistic instruction at the university level (Matsuda, 2006). Most respondents had two decades of teaching experience; therefore, there may not have been a strong emphasis on diversity issues and Black English dialect in their university programs twenty years ago (Ibarra, 2006).

7. No statistical significance exists between English/language arts teachers' grade level(s) taught and their perceptions of Black English usage. This finding may have resulted because most participants taught only one grade level, and their responses may have been based on a myopic view of teaching.

8. ELA teachers perceive habitual *be*, copula absence, and subject-verb disagreement as the top three Black English features most frequently evidenced in Black English-speaking students' writing. These results supported the findings of scholars regarding Black English speakers' perpetual use of these features (Green, 2002a; Labov, 1970; Mufwene et al., 1998; Smitherman, 2000). The findings implied that ELA teachers should particularly explore ways to assist BE speakers in these grammatical areas. This result may contain bias because participants chose from a partial list of common BE features.

9. ELA teachers seem to be most concerned with: (a) the need for Black English speakers to recognize the relevance of Standard English instruction, (b) the difficulty White ELA teachers face when teaching BE-speakers to use Standard English, and (c) the need to find a balance between enforcing Standard English and being culturally responsive to diverse learners. The overall theme from these findings corroborated the view that some African Americans may feel obligated to maintain their culture by not following so-called White or mainstream traditions, which may result in cultural clashes between some White teachers and their Black English-speaking students (Delpit, 1998; Ogbu, 2003).

10. ELA teachers who instruct Black English speakers desire training in contrastive analysis and code-switching in order to adequately assist students in becoming bidialectal, or knowing how to transition back and forth from Black English to Standard English. In addition, English/language arts teachers expressed a desire for research-based professional development workshops focused on how they may achieve a balance between Standard English enforcement and cultural appreciation. These findings supported the claims of scholars concerning the important roles that culturally responsive pedagogy and bidialectalism play in meeting the needs of

culturally diverse learners (Ball & Farr, 2003; Gay, 2000; Nieto, 1999).

11. Based on ELA teachers' advice, beginning teachers of Black English speakers should value students and remain patient and culturally sensitive when teaching Standard English. In addition, they should address linguistic differences progressively and tactfully. These findings supported the assertion that teachers should use constructive methods when teaching Standard English to BE speakers in order to avoid humiliating situations resulting from constant correction (Coelho, 2004; Delpit, 1998; Smitherman, 2000).

Implications for Educational Practice

Based on the results of the study, the following implications are provided for educational practice:

1. A need seems to exist for English/language arts (ELA) teachers to familiarize themselves with Black English dialect and African American culture in order to effectively communicate with and teach Black English speakers.

2. Universities and graduate teacher preparation programs may need to provide and require more linguistics courses in nonstandard English dialects in order to adequately prepare prospective teachers of Black English speakers.

3. School districts may benefit by assessing the extent to which ELA teachers have been trained in nonstandard English dialects and providing opportunities for professional development training in this area.

4. The findings from this study suggested that constant correction of Black English dialect inhibits student learning. In addition to the research literature which supports these findings, data analysis showed a statistically significant difference between

younger and older teachers regarding their tendency to disagree with constant correction of Black English usage. Therefore, it is recommended that teachers avoid constant correction of Black English usage altogether.

5. Data analysis showed a statistically significant difference between male and female ELA teachers regarding the challenge of teaching Standard English to Black English speakers. The findings suggested that male ELA teachers were more likely than female teachers to agree that teaching Standard English to BE speakers is a challenging task. Therefore, school districts may benefit by providing additive measures of support for male English/language arts teachers.

6. Based on the research findings, English/language arts teachers perceived *habitual be, copula absence,* and *subject-verb disagreement* as the features most frequently evidenced in BE-speaking students' written composition. Therefore, it is recommended that ELA teachers focus particularly on effective means of teaching mainstream uses of adverbial phrases, "to be" verbs, and subject-verb agreement to Black English speakers. For example, ELA teachers may employ instructional methods such as contrastive analysis and code-switching techniques in which students are able to compare Standard English and Black English usage (Ball & Farr, 2003; Green, 2002; Smitherman, 2000).

7. Based on participants' open-ended responses referring to the need for increased cultural awareness, it may be beneficial for ELA teachers to research Black English dialect and the culture of African American students. With this knowledge, ELA teachers may be able to communicate more effectively with BE speakers and correctly decipher between dialect differences and language deficits.

8. Based on the findings and research literature, it is recommended that future teacher preparation programs target research-based practices that will assist beginning English/language arts teachers. These programs may benefit by specifically focusing

on achieving a balanced approach to language arts instruction through cultural sensitivity and linguistic competence.

Recommendations for Future Research

Based on the findings of this study, the researcher offers the following recommendations for future research:

1. Conduct a mixed-method study with an interview component to obtain greater insight relative to English/language arts teachers' perceptions of Black English usage and its speakers.

2. Expand the number of participants and replicate the study with English/language arts teachers who teach high populations of Black English-speaking students in inner city and at-risk schools.

3. Conduct a similar study with state-by-state comparisons of English/language arts teachers' perceptions of Black English usage.

Chapter Summary

The majority of the sample in this study comprised middle-aged, White women with graduate degrees. These teachers had approximately two decades of teaching experience and no training in nonstandard English dialects. Statistically significant findings suggested that male ELA teachers were more likely than female ELA teachers to agree that teaching BE speakers is a challenging task. In addition, ELA teachers tended to disagree with constant correction of BE usage, although younger, less experienced teachers were more compelled to favor constant correction of the dialect.

Participants expressed a desire to find a balance between enforcing Standard (or Academic) English and maintaining cultural sensitivity. Findings revealed a need for ELA teachers to receive professional development training in Black English dialect and cultural awareness in order to more effectively teach Standard English to BE-speaking students. The next chapter offers additional scholarship for meeting the needs of linguistically diverse students and other learners through research-based and best practices in education.

CHAPTER FOUR

OTHER LEARNING FACTORS TO CONSIDER

Chapter Overview

Myriad factors influence how people learn, and people differ in the way they prefer to learn. Scholars and researchers have spent years studying varied modalities of learning to explain these phenomena and discover approaches for maximizing one's learning. Understanding the learning preferences and characteristics unique to African American learners continues to be essential when teaching this student population. Becoming adept with code-switching, contrastive analysis, and other strategies previously mentioned may yield favorable student outcomes. However, one size does not fit all. Employing these techniques alone may not guarantee success for all linguistically different students.

Although cultural sensitivity is paramount, staying current with educational research across a wide range of topics is important in order to glean additional information regarding best practices in teaching and learning. This chapter focuses on the importance of employing varied instructional approaches for advancing achievement for all students in general as teachers cater to diverse student populations. It aims to illustrate how teachers may better assist diverse learners through the added benefits of concepts such as Bloom's taxonomy of learning, brain-based research, multiple intelligences, and technology immersion.

Accommodating Standard English Language Learners

Research studies have shown that children who speak English as a second language (ESL) frequently achieve at lower levels than native English-speaking children, especially in language-related areas (Jax, 1988; Valdez-Pierce, 2003; Wrigley, 2000). As a result, the typical solution proposed to improve ESL students' proficiency in English has centered on second-language teaching techniques. Some educators have adopted these techniques to assist dialect speakers in mastering Standard English (Mufwene, 1999; Smitherman, 2000). Scholars have studied best practices for instructing and assessing diverse learners, which have often centered upon explicit teaching and the use of varied assessments.

Sheltered English Instruction and English Language Learners

One of the most popular instructional approaches to teaching English as a second language involves the use of sheltered English instruction. This approach aims to help English language learners (ELLs) acquire language proficiency while learning curricular content. The Sheltered Instruction Observation Protocol model, created in 1999, provides a structured framework based on the following components: (a) preparation, (b) building background, (c) comprehensible input, (d) strategies, (e) interaction, (f) practice/application, (g) lesson delivery, and (h) review and assessment (Echevarria, Vogt, & Short, 2004). This model emphasizes the preparation of clear learning objectives with explicit instructional delivery.

During instructional delivery, teachers adjust their speech and content text (as needed) to make certain English language learners comprehend what is being taught. The lesson is built upon students' background knowledge and experiences as teachers work to ensure at least 95% student engagement. When students are actively engaged in the learning process, they have the opportunity to apply newly acquired language skills and/or content knowledge. Students are afforded frequent opportunities for peer collaboration and hands-on learning as they complete activities for reading, writing, listening, and speaking. Teachers provide scaffolding and curricular spiraling, carefully guiding students as they repeat the study of learning objectives with increasing difficulty to promote higher levels of learning. At the conclusion of the lesson, teachers review and assess both content and language-related tasks to make certain students have mastered learning objectives.

Explicit Instruction

Deciding what content to include during lesson planning is central to the lesson cycle. However, the manner in which teachers deliver the instructional content may actually determine whether or not the teacher is successful in reaching the learner. With respect to African American students, Lisa Delpit (2006) argued that students performed poorly in school because teachers failed to explicitly explain the rules of participation in mainstream society.

Compelling evidence indicates that for struggling learners, systematic, explicit instruction may better serve their learning needs. Some educators agreed that implicit methods of classroom instruction may fail to effectively reach all students. In fact, research suggests that explicit methods may actually be more effective than implicit instruction for both English language learners and second-dialect speakers in reading, writing, and Standard English mastery (Bayley, 2009; Rickford & Wolfram, 2009). Explicit teaching includes techniques such as direct explanation, modeling, guided practice, feedback, and application (Dickson, Collins, Simmons, and Kame'enui, 1998). Teachers provide clear statements of objectives, demonstrations, examples and non-examples, and explanations of how new concepts relate to prior knowledge.

Teachers' use of explicit teaching techniques may yield improved performance particularly for Standard English language learners because these students tend to benefit from additional means of scaffolding (University of Texas Center for Reading and Language Arts, 2003). It is also important that teachers explicitly explain classroom rules and procedures, such as working in learning centers, disseminating classroom supplies, and working cooperatively with classmates. Tompkins (2003) maintained that creating such an environment makes children feel safe and more willing to take risks, which holds true especially for English language learners and struggling readers and writers (p. 13).

Differentiated Instruction

Differentiated instruction is another approach aimed at catering to students' varied learning modalities. During this process, teachers strategically plan and adjust instruction according to the needs of each student. Carol Ann Tomlinson (2003) asserted that teachers should focus on each student's needs according to readiness levels (knowledge and skills), interests, and learning profiles (how they learn best). Teachers focus on what all students must learn (content), how they will tailor instruction according to each student's needs (process), and how they will assess students' understanding of the content (products). Assessing students before, during, and after instruction allows teachers to tailor instructional materials according to each student's ability level. Teachers should use assessment data to guide the decision-making process for lesson planning and assignment of students to small groups. Assessing student progress regularly may help ensure flexible grouping so students are not limited to the same small groups.

As a caveat, teachers should consider the core purpose of differentiated instruction and not allow the process to become overwhelming. Although widely popular, differentiated instruction is not without its critics. Mike Schmoker (2010), a researcher, speaker, and educational consultant, insisted that ". . . with so many groups to teach, instructors found it almost impossible to provide sustained, properly executed lessons for every child or group—and in a single class period." He maintained that "good lessons start with a clear, curriculum-based objective and assessment, followed by multiple cycles of instruction, guided practice, checks for understanding . . . and ongoing adjustments to instruction" (pp. 22-23). Therefore, teachers should be judicious in how they plan and deliver instruction to meet each student's needs.

Assessments in the Classroom

Educators typically utilize formative, interim, and summative assessments to evaluate student learning. A summative assessment is a large-scale assessment usually administered statewide or nationwide as part of an accountability program (e.g., high stakes or standardized test). This type of assessment is used to evaluate students' learning at the end of unit of study or course. Formative assessments are small-scale assessments that are utilized to inform future classroom instruction. Interim assessments fall between these two types of assessments and are generally used to provide aggregate data to assist educators in making informed decisions in the classroom and beyond. Interim assessments may be used for purposes such as predicting how well students will perform on summative assessments or evaluating the level at which they met learning goals (Perie, Marion, & Gong, 2007).

The Wisconsin Center for Education Research (2009) maintained that a balanced assessment system includes all of these assessments. However, the authors emphasized the benefit of using formative assessments for English language learners because these assessments allow teachers to monitor student progress *during* the teaching and learning process. Formative assessments are not graded and involve both planned and unplanned strategies that teachers use during instruction in order to check for understanding, identify learning gaps, and adjust instruction to ensure students master learning objectives. Some examples of formative assessments include teacher feedback, exit slips, and observations.

Of course, there are times when assessments are needed for grading purposes. Multiple choice and other traditional tests have often served this purpose. However, scholars contend that such tests do not adequately assess the knowledge and abilities of language minority students. For this reason, they advocate the use of authentic or performance-based assessments, which offer more equitable solutions to assess student learning (Farr & Trumbull, 1997; Smitherman, 2000).

Authentic assessments are useful for *all* learners because they focus on higher order thinking and how well students are able to apply knowledge to real-world contexts. They allow multiple solutions to problems (not just one correct answer) and opportunities for extended time to complete assessments (as needed). For example, students who enjoy hands-on learning may benefit from authentic assessments such as research projects or exhibitions. Students who need more time to complete assignments may benefit from assessments that allow them to compile samples of their best work in portfolios to be reviewed over time (e.g., writing samples). Portfolio assessments allow both teachers and students to assess student growth over an extended period of time. When implementing authentic assessments, teachers should be mindful of the benefit of using rubrics for grading purposes. Rubrics are tools that inform students in advance of teacher expectations and the scoring criteria that will be utilized for grading.

Regardless of what type of assessment is implemented, all assessments should be aligned with standards-based curriculum (what students are expected to know and be able to do) and clear learning objectives. With respect to English language learners, the Wisconsin Center for Education Research (2009) added that assessments should focus on content knowledge and skills as well as language proficiency (how students use language to make meaning of the content). These assessments should target students' vocabulary usage, language control (e.g., subject/verb agreement), and the quality of speech or writing "to ensure the comprehensibility of the communication" (p. 3).

Standard English Teaching and Cultural Sensitivity

Teaching Standard English language learners (SELLs) to become proficient in a standard dialect necessitates quality instructional delivery coupled with specific knowledge and skills. Wong-Fillmore and Snow (2000) asserted that in order to effectively teach language proficiency, teachers need to become educational linguists who possess a solid knowledge-base and the skills related to language learning and success in school.

Second Language Teaching and African American Learners

Noma LeMoine (2001) recommended six principles for teachers of African American Standard English language learners that included:

1. Building their knowledge and understanding of nonstandard language and the students who speak them.

2. Integrating linguistic knowledge about [Black English dialect] into instruction.

3. Using second language acquisition methods to support student learning of mainstream school language and literacy.

111

4. Employing a balanced instructional approach to literacy that incorporates language experience, whole language/access to books, and phonics.

5. Infusing the history and culture of SELLs into the curriculum.

6. Considering the learning styles and strengths of SELLs in designing instruction. (pp. 176–177).

In short, Lemoine recommended that teachers familiarize themselves with Black English dialect and take into consideration the learning styles and cultural aspects of these Standard English language learners while using a balanced approach to literacy instruction. (Appendix C presents a snapshot of the author's suggested instructional framework for ensuring balanced literacy instruction. This section also includes an observation tool that outlines key components of a comprehensive literacy program administrators may look for when conducting classroom observations).

Reading and Writing Instruction

Tompkins (2003) maintained that effective teachers understand how students learn and how reading instruction in particular is influenced by four interrelated theories that include:

1. Constructivist—how active learners relate new information to prior knowledge and organize information in their schemata.

2. Interactive—how readers construct meaning using both textual information and background knowledge.

3. Sociolinguistic—how students use language to learn as well as communicate and share experiences with others (social interaction).

4. Reader Response—how readers create meaning as they read, whether through aesthetic reading (*living* the story) or efferent reading (simply recalling information from the story).

With this perspective, informed teachers understand how to plan reading instruction that allows students to interact and become actively engaged in meaningful learning experiences. Students are able to connect new concepts to prior knowledge through varied language experiences.

As teachers find ways to enhance reading instruction, they should be mindful that reading should always be accompanied with opportunities for writing. Connecting writing to reading helps promote not only greater language proficiency but also higher-level thinking skills (McGinley and Tierney, 1989). Writing activities should focus on different genres such as narrative, expository, persuasive, and descriptive.

Delpit (2006) recommended that teachers incorporate learning strategies appropriate for all populations of students. Delpit noted that in order to cater to the needs of Black English speakers, teachers should be culturally sensitive and respect the students' home language while recognizing the importance of Standard English usage in mainstream society. With regard to writing instruction, Delpit posits that the writing process approach generates problems for African American students because they create situations in which students ultimately find themselves held accountable for knowing a set of rules about which no one has ever directly informed them. Reyes (1992) contended that culturally and linguistically diverse learners lack the comfort of middle-class, White students in the experimentation with language necessary to fully engage in the writing process. As a result, these students need teachers to provide direct and explicit instruction rather than a "one size fits all" approach (Reyes, 1992, pp. 437-439). Therefore, infusing an ample amount of varied writing assignments is important in order for students to become more proficient using Standard English in written form. Tompkins (2003) maintained that ESL students learn best through writing activities because it allows them to better detect grammatical errors that they might otherwise overlook when speaking.

Literature. Fox (1992) and Smitherman (2000) emphasized the need for teachers, particularly writing teachers, to examine African

American literary theory for strategies of reading and interpreting African American student writing. This instructional approach allows teachers to instruct students using strategies that are free from a myopic understanding of dialect interference. Teachers employ strategies free from deficit theories of language by integrating literacy instruction with the experience and history of African Americans. Wheeler and Swords (2006) suggested using stories containing grammatical patterns most often used by students to enhance lessons through a contrastive analysis approach. These authors suggest using literature such as Patricia McKissack's (1986) *Flossie and the Fox*, which creatively illustrates the difference between formal English (Fox's speech) and informal English (Flossie's speech). Literature provides opportunities for teachers to engage in meaningful dialogue with students about the appropriateness of both formal and informal language usage (e.g., word choice) as well as the power of language in writing.

   Identifying similarities and differences. Perhaps some of the most widely used instructional strategies among teachers in recent years have been those discussed in Marzano, Pickering, and Pollock's (2001) book, *Classroom Instruction That Works*. Based upon a meta-analysis of numerous studies, Robert Marzano and colleagues identified nine instructional strategies with a high probability of enhancing student achievement for all students (in descending order of effectiveness): (a) identifying similarities and differences, (b) summarizing and note-taking, (c) reinforcing effort and providing recognition, (d) homework and practice, (e) non-linguistic representations, (f) cooperative learning, (g) setting objectives and providing feedback, (h) generating and testing hypotheses, and (i) cues, questions, and advance organizers. Of these nine strategies, allowing students to identify similarities and differences yielded the greatest percentile gain in terms of positively impacting student achievement.

   Identifying similarities and differences has long been recognized as an important cognitive process as well (Costa & Lowery, 1989). Providing students with the opportunity to identify similarities and differences allows them to engage in tasks such as comparing, classifying, creating metaphors, and creating analogies. As previously noted, when students are allowed to make decisions regarding when to use informal (e.g., *She be here*) or formal speech (e.g., *She is usually here*), they are able to make comparisons to determine which sentences are most appropriate for specific contexts. When teachers implement such types of instructional strategies, they open avenues to higher student achievement.

Journaling. Journaling is an excellent alternative to extensive writing exercises because it provides opportunities for students to write about teacher-assigned topics as well as other topics that cater to students' interests. Students may use journals in a variety of ways such as note-taking, writing about personal experiences, responding to literature, and writing stories. However, journal activities may be extended to provide more student engagement. For example, students may write short stories or poems to be read either aloud to the class or to the teacher during student-teacher conferences. In order to accommodate students who are uncomfortable with public speaking, teachers may permit students to choose their type of presentation. Allowing students to read their stories aloud may increase the possibility that they will be able to detect deviations from Standard English.

Dialogue journals. Some teachers have found dialogue journals to be useful especially when working with ESL students or Standard English language learners. Dialogue journals allow for student-teacher or student-student interaction in a non-threatening context (Linnell, 2010; Peyton, 1993). Students who are less proficient in Standard English are able to interact with others who are proficient in Standard English. For example, teachers may assign students to a partner (student or teacher) to share their feelings about a story, current event, or personal experience. Instead of communicating verbally, students are able to respond to his/her partner in written form. Consider the following example of a written exchange between students regarding their feelings about a natural disaster:

> Student #1 writes: *I felt sad when people lost their*
> *homes after the storm.*
> *How did you feel?*

> Student #2 (dialect speaker/ESL student) writes: *I sad too.*

As students become more comfortable with dialogue journals, teachers may use this activity to gradually reinforce the rules of Standard English. Teachers should use discretion when deciding how much flexibility students will have in their written exchanges (e.g., length of time to complete the exchange). When assigning journal exercises, teachers may facilitate the writing experience by emphasizing *quality* rather than quantity in student writing.

Daily oral language. Students may also benefit by participating in daily oral language (D.O.L.) activities, which are generally used as opening exercises. D.O.L. activities are useful because teachers are able to present short sentences (e.g., on an overhead projector) focused on specific grammatical patterns and rules (e.g., She *be* grocery shopping every *m*onday vs. She usually goes grocery shopping every Monday). In this example, the teacher is able to focus on: (a) Standard English concepts (habitual *be*), (b) capitalization for days of the week (Monday), and (c) punctuation (period at the end of the sentence). Focusing on specific Black English features in addition to other conventions daily allows students to feel less threatened because they may consider the activities as simply a part of their daily routine. In addition to such exercises, teachers should be mindful that dialect speakers may need multiple opportunities throughout the day to practice oral language development through reading and dialogue. Students should be invited to participate in meaningful class discussions about stories they have read. Researcher Mike Schmoker (2006) insists that students should be able to participate in "argumentative literacy" (p. 68) in which they are able to not only read but also defend their opinions about what they have read through dialogue as well as writing. Providing students with such opportunities assists with building oral language proficiency as well as critical thinking skills.

Literacy centers. Students may also benefit from literacy centers, which allow students to work individually or with peers to practice both oral and written language skills. Teachers prepare and model activities ahead of time according to Standard English language learners' needs. For example, teachers may create/provide stories that include both formal and informal uses of language. Dialect speakers may pair with student mentors to first take turns reading the story aloud. Then, the students may use contrastive analysis and code-switching techniques to rewrite informal text using formal language. An extension of the activity may require students to generate comprehension questions for other students to answer during their time at the center.

Teachers may create activities that target specific dialect features (e.g., consonant cluster reduction). For example, using index cards to write sentences that include formal and informal speech patterns may assist students with identifying differences between informal and formal speech. One side of an index card may reflect formal language (e.g., *The pencil is on the /desk/.*), while the other side reflects informal language (e.g., *The pencil is on the /des/.*). Students may read sentences to partners/mentors, targeting the sentence that is most appropriate for formal settings (i.e., Standard English).

Interactive writing. Interactive writing such as *sharing the pen* is useful particularly with younger students (Fountas & Pinnell, 1996). During this process, teachers and students take turns writing meaningful text for various purposes. For example, teachers may use chart pads to focus on conventions of print such as directionality (arrangement of text on a page), grammar, usage, punctuation, spelling, upper and lower case letters, spacing between words, and so forth. If mistakes are made, teachers and students are able to cover the mistakes with correction tape and make any necessary corrections. This collaborative process allows for immediate feedback and increased opportunities for student participation in writing.

Alternatives to extensive writing exercises. When determining which instructional practices to employ in classrooms, it is important that teachers take into account research-based and culturally sensitive practices aimed at achieving optimal learning outcomes. Geneva Smitherman (2000) suggested that English/ language arts teachers allow African American students to substitute some written work with activities such as improvisational drama, panel discussions, debates, and short speeches. Delpit (1998) also recommended techniques such as role playing, which teaches students that there are many ways to say the same thing and that certain contexts require particular kinds of linguistic performances. For example, teachers may allow students to create their own scripts and play roles as local news anchors or reporters. Using camcorders to record and review these performances may benefit students by allowing for both self and peer assessments. These types of activities allow students to recognize the importance of articulating words for their listeners. Students have the opportunity to practice Standard English usage such as adding the suffix –*ed* to certain words when referring to past events and keeping final consonant clusters, as discussed in chapter one.

Bloom's Taxonomy of Learning

In 1956, Benjamin Bloom, along with several other educators, developed one of the most respected and often cited taxonomies in education. Bloom and his colleagues created a framework commonly referred to as *Bloom's Taxonomy*, which addresses the cognitive (thinking), affective (feeling), and psychomotor (doing) domains (Bloom, Englehart, Furst, Hill, & Krathwohl, 1956). The group's aim was for educators to focus on all three domains to ensure a holistic approach to learning. Although much research has centered on these three domains, educators seem to most often refer to the cognitive domain when referencing ways to assist students in thinking at higher levels.

The cognitive domain in Bloom's taxonomy focuses on a hierarchy of mental processes. This domain allows educators to construct learning objectives that focus on higher order thinking. Bloom's original taxonomy included six levels of cognitive functioning: (a) knowledge, (b) comprehension, (c) application, (d) analysis, (e) synthesis, and (f) evaluation. The knowledge and evaluation levels represented the lowest and highest levels, respectively. In more recent years, Anderson and Krathwohl (2001) revised the taxonomy by replacing nouns with active verbs. The first four concepts in the revised taxonomy reflected the following: (a) *remember* (knowledge), (b) *understand* (comprehension), (c) *apply* (application), and (d) *analyze* (analysis). The authors also reversed the two highest levels (synthesis and evaluation) and renamed them *evaluating* (evaluation) and *creating* (synthesis), respectively. Huitt (2011) suggested that the two highest levels are virtually equal and interdependent; therefore, effectiveness is lost if one is omitted.

Each level serves as a springboard in reaching the next level to build students' capacity to think critically. For example, once students are able to recall (*remember*) a concept, they may be able to move on to higher levels of thinking in which they explain (*understand*), then demonstrate (*apply*), compare and contrast (*analyze*), make judgments (*evaluate*), and construct models (*create*) with respect to that concept. To help foster higher levels of thinking, teachers should transition from lower to higher level questioning. One way to accomplish this goal is to shift from simple recall questions (e.g., "Where did the story take place?") to higher order questions (e.g., "Why do you think the author chose this setting?"). Higher level questioning enables students to shift from using simple responses (e.g., "Pittsburg, Pennsylvania") to more complex responses (e.g., "The author chose this setting because . . ."). Teachers should encourage students to answer questions using complete sentences in order to strengthen oral language skills.

Teachers' use of higher-order questioning remains essential in sharpening critical thinking skills. However, class discussions should allow for student-generated as well as teacher-generated questions. Once teachers have modeled appropriate questioning techniques, students should be given ample opportunities to ask questions. As students become more comfortable with asking basic questions, they should be encouraged to begin questions with words such as *which, why,* and *how,* all of which focus on problem-solving. Higher-order questioning techniques provide opportunities for both critical thinking and students' ownership of their learning (Conklin, 2006; Costa & Lowery, 1989).

Teachers may also consider ways to ensure higher order thinking through higher level learning activities. For example, during Black History month, teachers typically celebrate the successes of numerous African Americans. One activity teachers might choose to incorporate is to discuss different African American inventors and allow students to *become* inventors. Students may be given the opportunity to either re-invent products or construct their own inventions to be put on display. Incorporating such activities and displaying student work may promote higher levels of thinking (*synthesis/create* level) as well as higher levels of students' self-esteem.

Brain-Based Learning

Research surrounding how the brain learns warrants extensive discussion because this is where all learning occurs. However, it is important for educators to first understand that the brain cannot focus on learning if basic needs are not met (Sousa, 2011). Abraham Maslow (1968) outlined basic needs for humanity: (a) physiological (e.g., food, shelter), (b) safety (e.g., security), (c) belonging and love (e.g., positive relationships), (d) esteem (e.g., self-respect, success), and (e) self-actualization (i.e., becoming what the individual is most suited for)—highest level on hierarchy.

Although teachers may not be able to meet all of students' basic needs (e.g., shelter), they are uniquely situated to help ensure certain needs are met within the classroom. When teachers establish a climate of trust and manage their classrooms well, students may inevitably feel a sense of safety and belonging. Making certain every student experiences success—whether by passing an exam, receiving a high five from the teacher, answering a question correctly, or simply feeling free from fear to ask questions—may help shield students from feelings of inadequacy and insecurity during the learning process. Helping to secure students' basic needs may assist teachers in minimizing distracters as they attempt to focus on instructional strategies that cater to the ever-learning brain.

Brain research posits that the human brain is constantly seeking patterns and searching for meaning, or seeking connections between the new and the known. The brain is composed of neurons which contain thousands of branches (or dendrites) emerging from its core. If knowledge is to increase, the neural networks must physically change. Neurons that are repeatedly used grow stronger synapses and more effective neural networks. The more they fire, the more they send out new dendrites looking for more new and useful connections. Cells that are not used are pruned away, leaving more room to add dendrites to the nerve cells that are used (Sousa, 2011).

Brain-based learning involves the use of instructional approaches that rely on current brain research to support and develop teaching strategies. In the classroom, teachers either cultivate students' dendrites or allow them to prune away. Brain researchers have concurred that if learning is to take place, and if teachers are to allow students' dendrites to grow, their lessons must be connected to emotion, meaning, and novelty (Sousa, 2011; Sprenger, 2005; Tate, 2003; Wolfe, 2001; Zull, 2002). In order to maximize learning, it is important to allow students to make connections between what is being taught, what they already know, and what is important to them.

Emotion

Emotion takes precedence over all other brain processes. The way people feel always influences the brain because emotion and thought are significantly intertwined (Zull, 2004). Teachers who use strategies that get students emotionally involved in the lesson are likely to enhance learning. Kochman's (1990) finding that African Americans tend to use more of an emotional and involving mode to excite their audiences suggests that many African Americans must feel emotionally attached to the lesson in order for their learning to be maximized. Showing enthusiasm, allowing for student choice, incorporating storytelling, and playing music are just a few examples of ways teachers may stimulate emotion to promote student learning (Sprenger, 2005).

Meaning

Meaning refers to the relevancy that students attach to new learning as they connect content to prior learning experiences. Neuroscientist and teacher Marilee Sprenger (2005) suggested making meaning by modeling concretely or symbolically and using examples from students' experiences. Incorporating students' experiences allows them to bring prior knowledge into working memory, which accelerates making sense of and attaching meaning to new learning. When it is not possible to identify examples from student experience to create meaning, teachers may resort to using memory aids such as mnemonic devices. Mnemonic devices assist students in connecting the new and the known. One way students may use the mnemonic device technique is to associate corresponding letters to new concepts to assist them in retaining what is being taught. For example, language arts teachers might use the mnemonic *T.I.M.E.* to explain that effective authors need *TIME* in order to write a good story: a *T*itle, *I*ntroduction, *M*iddle, and *E*nd).

It is important to note that working memory deals with concepts for a limited time, and the goal is for students' knowledge to transfer from working memory (temporary storage) to long-term memory. Therefore, teachers may also consider chunking content for increased student retention. Chunking involves a process in which the brain perceives several items of information as a single item.

David Sousa (2011) expounded upon the use of pattern chunking and categorical chunking. The pattern chunking technique occurs when one is able to discover patterns in content, such as grouping steps in a sequence. On the other hand, categorical chunking allows for the classification of large amounts of information such as identifying similarities and differences using Venn diagrams or tree diagrams to sort information. Chunking the most important parts of a lesson within a shorter period of time and allowing students multiple opportunities to practice or rehearse skills may yield increased student performance rather than presenting information to students over a longer period of time without as much practice. In fact, Sousa maintained that packaging lessons into 15-20 minute components will likely result in maintaining greater student interest than one 40-minute lesson.

Novelty

In addition to creating meaning and stimulating emotion, brain researchers recommended that classroom instruction also include *novelty*—something that the brain perceives as being different or unusual. Adding novelty to instruction involves not only communicating the relevance of learning objectives but also utilizing tactics such as humor, beginning lessons with strange facts, and playing music relevant to the lesson (Sousa, 2011, Sprenger, 2005).

Incorporating humor in the classroom may be particularly useful for all students, as it allows them to enjoy the method of instructional delivery while making connections to what is being taught. Exhibiting excitement and humor during the instructional phase allows students to become more engaged and feel that what they are learning is worthwhile. In a study conducted on teachers' influence on their students, Csikszentmihalyi and McCormack (1986) found that making learning enjoyable is extremely important in the learning process. The authors cited that 58% of study participants mentioned how one or more influential teachers made learning fun, and that one participant revealed, "After all these years, [she] found out for the first time that [she] really liked English" (p. 419).

Nonlinguistic Representations

The use of visual or nonlinguistic representations plays an important role in promoting learning because 84% of all information that comes to the brain is visual (Jensen, 1998). Graphic organizers and other visual tools help stimulate learning as students attempt to process new information. For example, the Frayer Model is particularly useful when teaching new vocabulary terms to dialect speakers and other students. It provides a visual tool that requires students to provide definitions, characteristics, examples, and non-examples of new terms. This model lends itself to the contrastive analysis technique because it enables teachers to extend usage of the model to define concepts as well as exhibit examples and non-examples of Standard English usage. Figure 4.1 shows how a teacher might use the Frayer Model to define singular possessive nouns while comparing and contrasting formal (F) and informal (I) variations. When using the model, teachers may remind students that Standard English (SE) is used for formal settings; therefore, the informal or dialect variation is used as a non-example.

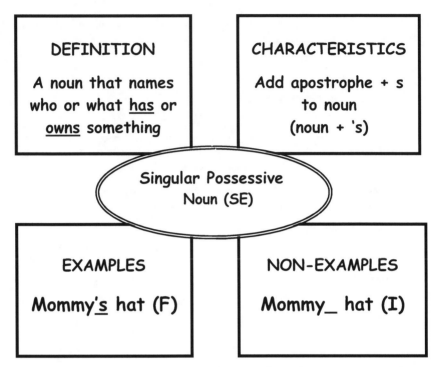

DEFINITION

A noun that names
who or what <u>has</u> or
<u>owns</u> something

CHARACTERISTICS

Add apostrophe + s
to noun
(noun + 's)

Singular Possessive
Noun (SE)

EXAMPLES

Mommy<u>'s</u> hat (F)

NON-EXAMPLES

Mommy_ hat (I)

Figure 4.1. Frayer Model used to define singular possessive nouns

Word walls also serve as excellent visual tools because they provide visual scaffolding for students to assist them in making the transition to more independent reading and writing (Rycik, 2002). Word walls are organized collections of words that are usually considered *non-negotiable*, and students are expected to use and spell them correctly in their writing. Generally, teachers select words from reading programs, high-frequency word lists, irregular words, and commonly used words that students use in their reading and writing.

In addition to using a word wall, teachers may want to consider implementing a *speech* wall that focuses specifically on formal and informal uses of language. Speech walls may be used in much the same way as word walls are used in the classroom. For example, word walls serve as immediately accessible dictionaries for the most troublesome words (Cunningham & Allington, 1999, p. 140). Likewise, teachers should ensure that examples posted on speech walls target informal language most often used by the majority of the dialect speakers in the classroom (e.g., double negatives). Some of the most salient guidelines include:

1. Labeling and neatly placing walls in highly visible and clearly defined places in the classroom.

2. Ensuring wall content is based on student needs.

3. Ensuring wall content is added gradually (not all at once).

4. Interacting with students regarding specific concepts (e.g., language differences) *before* placing content on the wall.

5. Encouraging students to refer to the wall when needed (e.g., formal writing assignments).

Sentence strips may be used to post examples of informal and formal language to help students distinguish between both uses of language. Teachers should emphasize that the formal uses of language are non-negotiable for tests and other assignments that require Standard English usage. Notice in Figure 4.2 how the speech wall provides examples of informal speech being translated into formal speech.

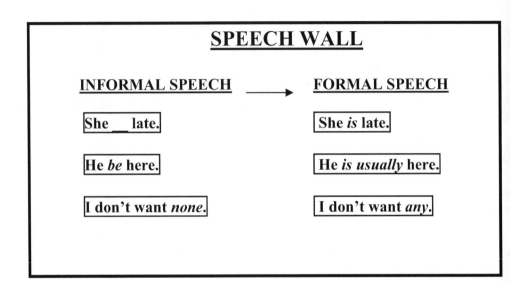

Figure 4.2. Speech wall used to distinguish between informal and formal uses of language

As with word walls, speech walls may be personalized to meet student needs. For students who have not yet mastered specific learning objectives, file folders may be used to make *portable* speech walls to be kept at students' desks for immediate access. Students may refer to the classroom speech wall or their personal speech walls for purposes such as editing formal writing assignments.

Primacy-Recency Effect

Another pertinent point to remember is the Primacy-Recency Effect. This concept suggests that during learning episodes, students tend to remember best that which comes at the beginning, second best that which comes at the end, and least that which comes just past the middle (Sousa, 2011; Tate, 2003). Beginning and ending each lesson with memorable events is central to helping students better retain what has been taught. Sousa (2011) outlined key lesson components to take into account when planning lessons:

1. Explicit teaching or modeling (enhances sense and meaning)

2. Checking for understanding (e.g., Bloom's comprehension level)

3. Guided practice (e.g., Bloom's Application level)

4. Closure (last chance to attach sense and meaning and thus improve retention)

5. Independent practice (helps students make new learning permanent)

Although educators' views may differ regarding when to implement each component (e.g., closure before or after independent practice), fundamental concepts should be retained. Once teachers have explicitly taught a lesson with modeling, students complete assignments with teacher assistance. After students exhibit basic understanding, they should be given multiple opportunities for independent practice to maximize learning. In fact, research indicated that allowing students to practice or rehearse skills repeatedly resulted in a 21-44% gain in student learning (Marzano, Pickering, & Pollack, 2001).

Metacognitive Strategies

Teachers should consider maximizing students' learning by providing them with opportunities to employ meta-cognitive strategies in which they "think about their thinking." Teachers should first model the use of metacognitive strategies before students attempt to use them. Although there are various ways to use metacognitive strategies, teachers may be creative when using these strategies to teach Standard English to dialect speakers. For example, teachers may choose specific sentences from a story and verbalize how they might use code-switching if they were in a formal setting. In her book, *Pink and Say*, Patricia Polacco (1994) uses examples from Black English when Pink (a Black union soldier) speaks in the story. When Pink discovers and rescues Say (another soldier who is left for dead), he asks, "Where you hit?" Teachers may use these types of sentences to model how they would use metacognitive strategies (or think aloud) to translate the sentence into

Standard English. In addition to using metacognitive strategies during whole group instruction, students should also have the opportunity to use these and other strategies as they work in collaborative groups with their peers. Because the brain is innately social and collaborative, permitting students to work in cooperative learning groups facilitates the learning process (Wolfe, 2001).

While much is yet to be known about how the brain learns, it is important that teachers become knowledgeable about the research surrounding the positive impact that novelty, emotion, and meaning have on student learning. With respect to African American students, this research clearly corroborates Boykin's (1986) delineation of the African American cultural experience, such as their proclivity for music, social bonds, and novelty. When teachers promote brain-based learning and infuse African American culture in classroom instruction, they allow for increased motivation among African American students. This approach permits meaning-making experiences for students through cultural sensitivity. These types of authentic learning situations increase the brain's ability to make connections and retain new information.

Howard Gardner's Theory of Multiple Intelligences

Howard Gardner (1983) defined intelligence as one's ability to: (a) solve real-life problems, (b) generate new problems to solve, and (c) create products or offer services that are valued within one's culture or community. Gardner insisted that intelligence does not focus on how smart one is but rather *how one is smart*. In his research, Gardner (1983) theorized that individuals possess seven multiple intelligences, with certain intelligences being more developed than others: Verbal-linguistic, Intrapersonal, Logical-mathematical, Interpersonal, Musical, Bodily-kinesthetic, and Spatial. After conducting additional research, Gardner (1999) later introduced Naturalist, Existential, and Spiritual intelligences. In order to assist the reader in remembering these intelligences, the author provides a mnemonic device (*V.I.N.E. L.I.M.B.S.S.*) along with encapsulations of how they apply to student learning as per Conklin (2006) and Gardner (1999, 2010):

1. *V* erbal-linguistic—Students enjoy working with words.

2. *I* ntrapersonal—Students enjoy working individually.

3. *N* aturalistic—Students enjoy outdoor experiences.

4. *E* xistential—Students enjoy asking deep questions (e.g., "What is love?").

5. *L* ogical-mathematical—Students are interested in numbers, etc.

6. *I* nterpersonal—Students enjoy working in groups.

7. *M* usical—Students enjoy singing, playing instruments, etc.

8. *B* odily-kinesthetic—Students enjoy hands-on activities.

9. *S* patial—Students enjoy drawing, creating projects, etc.

10. *S* piritual—Students are interested in the mysteries and meanings of life (e.g., "Where do we come from?").

Reflecting on 25 years of his research on multiple intelligences, Gardner (2010) rejected the misconception that these proposed intelligences are *learning styles*. Instead, Gardner analogized each of the multiple intelligences to individual computers, explaining that "computers work more or less well." Gardner also outlined two educational premises for educators to consider: (a) Individualizing—learning as much as possible about each learner, teaching in a variety of ways to reach all learners, and assessing in ways that allow learners to show what they understand and (b) Pluralizing—Deciding what is most important and teaching in a variety of ways to address the different intelligences. Gardner maintained that teaching in many ways allows teachers to reach more students because once they understand something well, it allows them to conceive the concept in various ways (i.e., dramatizations, illustrations, categorizations, etc.).

One of the goals of education is to assist in the development of well-rounded individuals. Therefore, it may benefit teachers to focus on targeted learning objectives and determine the most effective ways to incorporate multiple intelligence theory when teaching those objectives.

Infusing Technology in the Classroom

As teachers consider various alternatives to teaching all learners, it is also important to be mindful of the benefits of using technology in every classroom. Many students have become increasingly acclimated to our ever-growing digital age. New technologies such as iPods and MP3 players, digital Tablet PCs (or tablet computers), and Smartphones have become progressively popular in recent years. Some students may occupy much of their time with digital devices, whether sending text messages to friends on feature phones or Smartphones, downloading and listening to music on MP3 players, or simply pairing with friends to play Wi-Fi (wireless fidelity) video games.

Over the years, technological advancements have made it possible for educators and other professionals to become more efficient in their line of work. For example, Smartphones alone allow users to easily access email, send and receive text messages, schedule meetings, or find specific locations when traveling using its GPS (Global Positioning System) navigation capabilities. Instead of toting loads of books, professionals are now able to download and read multiple e-books on Tablet PCs and other mobile devices. Likewise, students should be afforded similar opportunities because technology is an "integral part of the students' quest for knowledge and a tool through which students research, organize, and share information" (Johnston & Cooley, 2001, p. 25).

Although it may not be practical to integrate every technological tool that becomes available, teachers may choose devices that are most useful in their classrooms. Oftentimes, students may use desktop or laptop computers to browse the internet for research projects, use interactive software to practice specific skills, and so forth. However, mobile devices such as Tablet PCs may provide additional benefits because they function like desktop and laptop computers but are lightweight and require less space for storage. With the help of digital pens, students may use digital tablets for journaling, note-taking, and other writing purposes. Teachers may also browse the internet for mobile applications (mobile apps) that may be downloaded for educational purposes (e.g., writing or grammar activities). Students may also use digital tablets to download e-books for reading assignments. Tablet PCs and digital pens also allow teachers to have interactive lessons in which they are able to walk around the classroom and use projector screens to display what they write on the tablet.

Some computer programs have existed for quite some time but are still useful today. For example, Microsoft PowerPoint was first introduced over 20 years ago, yet it remains an excellent resource for oral presentations. Teachers may group students heterogeneously and allow them to create PowerPoint presentations, which encourages creativity and collaboration. Heterogeneous grouping further enhances the activity because it provides opportunities for higher performing students to assist Standard English language learners in organizing sentences and identifying grammatical and other errors. If available, students may use Smartboards (interactive whiteboards) or projector screens to display PowerPoint presentations.

Teachers may keep current with modern technology through professional development opportunities or through collaboration among colleagues. As technology continues to grow exponentially, it is incumbent upon teachers to become technology savvy in order to be better prepared to meet the needs of all students. Whenever possible, students should be exposed to technology-infused environments to enhance learning experiences.

Chapter Summary

Effective Standard English instruction involves the junction between cultural awareness and sound instructional practices. When teachers implement research-based strategies and consider creative alternatives when teaching linguistically different learners, they allow for not only increased student engagement but also optimal academic achievement. The final chapter emphasizes the importance of equipping prospective teachers with the necessary knowledge and skills to become effective classroom teachers. It also underscores the important role that all stakeholders play in providing the impetus to promote continuous improvement in the educational system.

CHAPTER FIVE

WHERE DO WE GO FROM HERE?

Chapter Overview

Across the nation, many teachers face the challenge of arresting the longstanding achievement gap between linguistically different African American learners and their mainstream peers. The overall success of Black English speakers depends largely upon their teachers' ability to successfully plan and deliver instruction through the acquisition of effective pedagogical skills.

Educators often emphasize the importance of teachers receiving professional development training *during* their full-time teaching experience. However, this chapter begins with a discussion of the importance of equipping prospective teachers with the tools necessary to meet the demands of a diverse student population *before* they enter the teaching profession. Of course, teachers alone will not solve all of the problems plaguing public education today. The chapter concludes with a call for all key stakeholders to make a concerted effort in taking responsibility for procuring the most effective practices that will ensure student success.

Teacher Preparation Programs

For several years, educators and researchers have sought to determine which school variables have the greatest influence on student achievement. Since the early 1990s, researchers have documented a close relationship between teaching quality and student achievement. The National Council for Accreditation of Teacher Education [NCATE] (2010) agreed that ". . . research over the past decade indicates that no *in-school* intervention has a greater impact on student learning than an effective teacher (p. 1)." Having an effective teacher in the classroom greatly impacts student achievement, especially for low-income and minority students (Nye, Konstantopoulos, & Hedges, 2004; Sanders & Rivers, 1996). Research shows that teachers' effectiveness is strongly related to the preparation they receive for teaching (Darling-Hammond & Youngs, 2002; Ferguson, 1991).

Preparing prospective teachers before they enter the full-time teaching profession may result in heightened student performance. In a study to examine the ways in which teacher qualifications and other school inputs related to student achievement, Darling-Hammond (2000b) found that teacher quality characteristics were significantly and positively correlated with student outcomes. Characteristics such as education level (percentage of teachers with master's degrees) showed positive but less strong relationships with education outcomes. Darling-Hammond found that teacher preparation and certification were the strongest correlates of student achievement in reading and mathematics both before and after controlling for student poverty and language status.

In 2003, the International Reading Association conducted a study of exemplary teacher preparation programs and identified eight essential features needed in reading teacher education programs (Edwards, McMillon, and Turner (2010):

1. Content—comprehensive curriculum to help pre-service teachers enhance their knowledge base

2. Apprenticeship—course-related field experiences with opportunities for pre-service teachers to interact with exceptional mentors

3. Vision—a shared view of quality literacy teaching and learning

4. Resources and mission—adequate resources to support the teacher preparation program's mission

5. Personalized teaching—a pedagogical approach focused on student diversity and commitment to student learning

6. Autonomy—allowing teachers to take ownership in decision-making

7. Community—active partnerships between faculty, students, and mentor teachers

8. Assessment—ongoing assessment of students and content with opportunities for programmatic changes as needed

In accordance with these findings, the National Research Council (2010) identified three aspects of teacher preparation "that are likely to have the highest potential for effects on outcomes for students:" (a) content knowledge, (b) quality of teacher candidates, and (c) field experiences (p.180). Building upon these findings, NCATE (2010) convened and supported the work of a Blue Ribbon panel of experts to develop a plan directed toward turning teacher education "upside down." This diverse group included teachers, educational leaders, state officials, teacher educators, union representatives, and critics of teacher education. The plan called for increased accountability in which: (a) teacher education programs are "fully grounded in clinical practice and interwoven with academic content and professional courses," (b) there is shared responsibility of teacher education where higher education institutions partner with school districts to redesign teacher education programs to better support prospective teachers, and (c) state policies provide incentives for such partnership arrangements along with the elimination of any legal or regulatory barriers (iii).

The Blue Ribbon panel recognized "the urgent need to address the staffing and learning challenges facing high-need and low-performing schools." The group called for state policymakers to "revamp teacher licensing requirements by raising expectations for graduates of teacher preparation programs" (NCATE, 2010, pp. iv-v). The panel recommended that the U.S. Department of Education and federal lawmakers invest funds for school improvement efforts and continue providing grant funds for school and university partnerships. The group maintained that in order for the nation to be competitive in this global economy, our teachers "will have to educate all students—including those from increasingly diverse economic, racial, linguistic, and academic backgrounds—to the same high learning outcomes" (NCATE, 2010, p. 1).

This robust call to action offers promising results for our future generation. It recognizes the importance of strengthening teacher education programs through the lens of real-world, effective practices focused on diversity. As Ball and Farr (2003) noted, if teacher education programs focus on combating cultural conflicts, it may contribute to positive long-term change. Educators agreed that in order to improve the academic performance of African American students, teacher education programs should ensure that teachers acquire an elevated level of authentic knowledge of African American culture. These programs should emphasize the impact that African American culture has on student behavior, learning styles, and preferred teaching styles (Berry, 2003; Ogbu, 2003; Smitherman, 2000). With respect to dialect speakers, it is particularly important that teacher education programs include curricula that focus specifically on language awareness.

Oubre (1997) maintained that the goal of enhancing teacher awareness and understanding of the sociolinguistic and historical roots of Black English dialect is ultimately to improve the classroom situation for students. In order to accomplish this goal, it is essential for prospective teachers to understand that language plays an important role in the teaching and learning process. According to Reagan (2005), students in public schools who were speakers of Black English continued to be disproportionately misdiagnosed and mislabeled with respect to both cognitive and speech or language problems. Reagan contended that this fact alone constituted a justification for additional teacher preparation relative to language differences.

Some linguists cited English/language arts teachers as lacking linguistic competence, frequently mistaking dialect miscues as grammatical errors. They argued that school districts still infrequently hired linguists, and teacher training programs seldom offered linguistics courses (Baugh, 1998, 2000; Cullinan, 1974; Cunningham, 1976; Delpit, 1995; Green, 2002a). Matsuda (2006) added that college programs were ill-prepared to meet the needs of second-language writers because few graduate programs offered courses on language issues, and even fewer programs required such courses.

Teacher preparation programs are responsible for ensuring that prospective teachers obtain the knowledge, skills, and dispositions needed to become effective classroom teachers. These programs should allow prospective teachers to focus on a comprehensive curriculum and work actively with mentor teachers in diverse settings. Curricular activities should focus on fundamental subject matter as well as student culture, language, and linguistics. When pre-service teachers are immersed in cultural awareness activities in the college classroom and throughout their field experiences, it allows for increased chances they will become more adequately prepared to teach diverse learners.

The Blue Ribbon panel appealed to all key stakeholders to join in the effort and recognize that "our economic future depends on our ability to ensure that all teachers have the skills and knowledge they will need to help their students overcome barriers to their success . . ." (NCATE, 2010, p. v). Failing to provide teachers with the tools they need to become effective educators could ultimately lead to pervasive inopportunity for many students.

Retaining Quality Teachers

When teacher preparation programs emphasize the importance of knowing what and how to teach students through culturally sensitive practices, the intent is to empower prospective teachers to become better prepared to meet the needs of diverse learners. However, the challenge remains to keep effective teachers in the classroom. The challenge is even greater when considering new teachers who are at greater risk of leaving the profession within the first five years of teaching.

Darling-Hammond and Sykes (2003) found that one of the primary causes for teachers leaving the profession is a lack of support. As teachers continue to leave the profession within the first several years of teaching, school leaders should work to identify and combat factors that lead to teacher attrition. The Alliance for Excellent Education (2004) posited that providing comprehensive induction in the form of mentoring, formal assessments, professional development and support for teachers during their first two years helps maximize teacher retention.

During an era when America's student population is becoming increasingly multicultural, its teaching workforce reflects a trend in the opposite direction. Besides the growing number of minority students, the proportion of minority teachers has remained relatively steady in recent years. Although minority teachers have entered the profession at higher rates than White teachers over the past 20 years, there has also been a higher rate of attrition among minority teachers. For the 2008-2009 school year, minority students comprised 41% of the elementary and secondary student population, whereas minority teachers comprised 16.5% of the elementary and secondary teachers (Ingersoll & May, 2011). These statistics suggest that many minority students may not receive instruction from role-model minority teachers who may have an advantage in discovering the most effective ways to teach students who are experiencing difficulty in school (Cavazos, 2002). Ensuring that teachers (especially minority) have the opportunity to participate in the decision-making process is extremely important to the overall success of the school (Ingersoll, 2007). Ingersoll and May (2011) reported that the greatest factors that influenced minority teachers' decision to leave the profession involved their level of autonomy regarding classroom and school-wide decision-making.

Capitalizing on Stakeholder Groups

Meeting the needs of diverse student populations is not the sole responsibility of the classroom teacher. This task warrants the assistance of all stakeholders working toward a common goal—success for all. The attainment of this goal is not marked by intermittent attempts to achieve short-term gains but by goal-directed practices coupled with continuous monitoring and a commitment to long-term solutions.

Capturing input from diverse stakeholders is integral in order to accomplish systemic goals and maintain long-term support. When forming stakeholder teams, it is important to make certain all students are well represented. Each student ethnic group should be represented by at least one member of the stakeholder team who is of the same ethnicity. Stakeholder teams may consist of school administrators, teachers, counselors, parents, students, community members, and others who have a genuine interest in heightening student performance.

When both internal and external stakeholders become involved in the decision-making process, it "sends the message that what students learn and how well they learn it isn't an issue just for teachers and administrators but is a real priority for the community as well" (Wright & Saks, 2000). This approach is healthy for school organizations because it paves the way for greater tolerance and appreciation of cultural differences.

Professional Learning Communities

Schools have much latitude in the way they choose to organize stakeholder meetings. However, scholars contend that one of the most effective means of working toward the goal of continuous improvement is through the use of professional learning communities (PLCs). In his book, *Results Now*, Mike Schmoker (2006) suggested that engaging in professional learning communities represents one of the surest ways schools may experience dramatic improvement.

Richard Dufour (2004) explained that schools which adopt the guiding principles of professional learning communities: (a) ensure that students learn, (b) provide a culture of collaboration, and (c) focus on results. All stakeholders work together and assume responsibility for student learning. Professional learning communities identify students' current levels of achievement, establish goals to bolster student achievement, work collaboratively to achieve those goals, and monitor progress regularly. With respect to struggling students, the professional learning community's response is:

- Timely—school quickly identifies struggling students.

- Based on intervention—school provides *immediate* assistance for students experiencing difficulty.

- Directive—school requires that students receive additional educational assistance until they have mastered objectives. (pp. 6-10)

Stakeholders should first create an action plan that targets specific goals and objectives focused on student learning. The plan should identify the concepts students are required to learn, means of determining whether students have learned those concepts, and response measures that will need to be in place when students experience difficulty in learning. The plan should include continuous monitoring of both successes and challenges regarding student performance.

In carrying out the plan, schools may form data analysis teams that will be responsible for compiling specific data for all members of the team. Stakeholders may then analyze multiple measures of data that focus on key areas such as staff and student attendance, state and national student assessment scores by subgroup, graduation rates, and dropout rates. Data that provide insight into mastery of targeted objectives is useful for informing team members about areas requiring the most attention. Analyzing data and monitoring progress regularly strengthens systemic efforts by allowing stakeholders to engage in meaningful dialogue and make data-driven decisions.

Stakeholders should meet regularly to strategically plan for the success of all students. However, using other means such as email, focus groups, surveys, and public forums allows for additional feedback from stakeholders who may be unable to attend meetings on a regular basis. When stakeholders work collaboratively and value everyone's opinions, they are able to build upon the collective strength of the group and thus yield increased student achievement.

Forging Parent-School-Community Partnerships

The National PTA (1998) maintained that the most accurate predictor of student achievement is the extent to which families are able to create and encourage home learning environments, communicate high expectations, and become involved in their children's education at school as well as at home. Past research has shown that parental involvement has the potential to positively influence students' grades, attendance, retention rates, behavior, and overall attitude toward school. However, the impact may be even greater when schools, parents, and the wider community work to build a guiding coalition to further enhance student performance (Barton, 2003; Belfield & Levin, 2007; Bryan & Henry, 2008; Taylor, Pearson, Clark, & Walpole, 2000). As schools work to build strong parent-school-community partnerships, educators should focus on six types of involvement (Epstein et al., 2002):

1. Parenting—providing activities that assist parents in developing effective parenting skills.

2. Communicating—providing two-way communication with parents regularly through means such as newsletters, memos, and parent-teacher conferences regarding student progress, school functions, and other relevant issues.

3. Volunteering—encouraging parents to become actively involved as a school volunteer wherever applicable.

4. Learning at home—providing many opportunities for interactive homework between parents and children.

5. Decision-making—inviting parents to become involved in the decision-making process regarding school policies and procedures.

6. Collaborating with community—inviting other community members to become actively engaged in school activities and the decision-making process to promote student success.

Throughout the school year, schools typically hold events such as open house, parent-teacher conferences, family night events, and other school functions in which parents are able to meet with teachers and become acquainted with curriculum and other aspects of the school. During this time, school leaders and teachers should endeavor to make parents feel that they are always welcome and that the school has their children's best interest at heart. At the beginning of the year, teachers should take steps to learn as much about their students as possible and work to build a high level of trust with both parents and students. Teachers should communicate with parents regularly throughout the school year about what their children will be learning and how well they are performing in class. If concerns arise regarding a student's behavior or academic performance, teachers should make parents aware of their concerns while also communicating positive aspects about the student.

School leaders should be mindful that some parents may need opportunities to familiarize themselves with school curriculum in order to better assist their children with assignments at home. Incorporating various curricular events throughout the year allows educators to share goals and expectations with parents regarding what students will be learning in school. For example, schools may hold a family literacy night in which teachers share learning objectives and strategies that parents may use when helping their children with reading and writing activities at home. It may also be beneficial to share research with parents regarding the strong correlation between parental involvement and higher student performance. With respect to reading literacy, parent involvement research has shown that when parents and children work together on reading activities, children's language and reading skills improve significantly from preschool to high school (Sheldon & Epstein, 2005). Schools should also inform the business community of school events and recruit volunteers. Some business leaders may even be willing to contribute door prizes, which may be used as incentives to boost participation rates.

Schools should use positive means of communicating to parents about important topics that impact their children's education. Because of the strong correlation between student achievement and parental involvement, educators should welcome feedback from parents and encourage them to become actively involved with school organizations such as the Parent Teacher Association (PTA) and other committees.

Schools should keep parents informed of important stakeholder meetings and invite them to participate regularly in the school's decision-making process in order to continuously communicate the important role that parents play in their children's lives.

Our Journey Upward

In 2009, United States President Barack Obama and Secretary of Education Arne Duncan launched the *Race to the Top* initiative to promote education innovation and reform. The $4.35 billion competitive grant program was designed to reward states that served as models in demonstrating success in essential areas such as raising student achievement, closing achievement gaps, and improving high school graduation rates.

Some educators may agree that the push for more palpable reform in education among America's schools could not have come at a better time. That same year, the Programme for International Student Assessment (PISA) conducted an international assessment among 34 countries included in the Organization for Economic Cooperation and Development (OECD). The PISA assessment is administered every three years and assesses 15-year-old students' knowledge and skills in reading, science, and mathematics, with a particular focus on one of the subjects in depth. Reading literacy was the major focus of study for that year.

After the 2009 PISA assessment results were tallied, the OECD (2011) reported that the United States had ranked average in both reading (14th) and science (17th) and below average in mathematics (25th). According to the results for reading literacy, White (525) and Asian (541) students scored higher than the overall OECD (493) and U.S. (500) averages; however, African American (441) and Hispanic (466) students' scores fell well below these averages (Fleischman, Hopstock, Pelczar, & Shelley, 2010).

In response to similar results from the previous 2006 PISA assessment, Darling-Hammond (2010) challenged the nation to ratchet up efforts to assist the increasing number of minority students and English language learners because the overall success of our nation would ultimately hinge upon their academic performance. She explained how White and Asian students scored above the national average in each

143

subject area but after adding the scores of African American and Hispanic students, the U.S. national average "plummets to the bottom tier of the rankings" (p. 11).

Seeing that the overall ranking of the United States is greatly impacted by the academic performance of each student subgroup, our mission continues in reshaping American schools to meet the needs of all students. If the United States is to become a model leader in education, it is incumbent upon educational leaders and all stakeholders to work together and engage in meaningful dialogue that takes into account the academic needs of diverse learners. However, in order to engage in meaningful conversations, one must first know how to converse. Without the ability to speak in ways that cater to the listener, how will these conversations begin? If mainstream teachers are unable to understand dialect speakers, how will they effectively teach *all* students? If dialect speakers are unable to understand mainstream teachers, how will *all* students learn? In our quest to race to the top in this global competition, we may ultimately overcome obstacles to high academic achievement for all by first revving up our efforts to *overcome language barriers*. So, what are we waiting for? The race is on!

ON YOUR MARK . . . GET READY. . . GET SET . . . GO!

References

Abdul-Alim, J. (2010). *Report: U.S. schools failing to educate Black males.* Retrieved from http://diverseeducation.com/article/14044/report-u-s-k-12-schools-failing-to-educate-black-males.html

Anderson, L.W., & Krathwohl, D. (Eds.). (2001). *A taxonomy for learning, teaching, and assessing: A revision of Bloom's taxonomy of educational objectives.* New York: Longman.

Ary, D., Jacobs, L., & Razavieh, A. (1996). *Introduction to research in education.* (5th ed.). Fort Worth, TX: Holt, Rinehart, and Winston, Inc.

Asante, M. (1998). *The Afrocentric idea.* Philadelphia: Temple University Press.

Avruch, K. & Black, P. (1993). Conflict resolution in intercultural settings. In D. J. D. Sandole & H. van der Merwe (Eds.), *Conflict resolution theory and practice* (pp. 131-145). Manchester, U.K.: Manchester University Press.

Babbie, E. (1990). *Survey research methods* (2nd ed.). Belmont, CA: Wadsworth Publishing Company.

Bailey, B. (1965). A new perspective in American Negro dialectology. *American Speech, 11*(1), 1-11.

Bailey, G., & Thomas, E. (1998). Some aspects of African American vernacular English phonology. In S. Mufwene, J. Rickford, G. Bailey, & J. Baugh (Eds.), *African American English: Structure, history, and use* (pp. 85-109). New York: Routledge.

Baldwin, J. (1979). If Black English isn't a language, then tell me, what is? Retrieved from http://www.nytimes.com/books/98/03/29/specials/baldwin-english.html.

Ball, A. (1992). Cultural preference and the expository writing of African American adolescents. *Written Communication, 9*(4), 501-532.

Ball, A. (1994). Investigating language, learning, and linguistic competence of African-American children: Torrey revisited. *Linguistics and Education, 7*(1), 23-46.

Ball, A. (1997). Expanding the dialogue on culture as a critical component when assessing writing. *Assessing Writing, 4*(2), 169-202.

Ball, A. (1998). Evaluating the writing of culturally and linguistically diverse students: The case of the African American Vernacular English speaker. In C. R. Cooper & L. Odell (Eds.), *Evaluating writing: The role of teachers' knowledge about text, learning, and culture* (pp. 225-248). Urbana, IL: National Council of Teachers of English Press.

Ball, A., & Farr, M. (2003). Language varieties, culture, and teaching the English language arts. In J. Flood, D. Lapp, J. R. Squire, & J. M. Jensen (Eds.), *Handbook of research on teaching the English language arts* (2nd ed., pp. 435-445). Mahwah, NJ: Erlbaum.

Banks, J. A., Cookson, P., Gay, G., Hawley, W. D., Irvine, J. J., Nieto, S., Schofield, J.W., & Stephan, W.G. (2001). Diversity within unity: Essential principles for teaching and learning in a multicultural society. *Phi Delta Kappan, 83*(3), 196-202.

Barton, P. (2003). *Parsing the achievement gap: Baselines for tracking progress.* Princeton, NJ: Policy Information Report, Educational Testing Service.

Baugh, J. (1998). Linguistics, education, and the law: Educational reform for African American language minority students. In S. Mufwene, J. Rickford, G. Bailey, & J. Baugh (Eds.), *African American English: Structure, history, and use* (pp. 282-301). New York: Routledge.

Baugh, J. (2000). *Beyond Ebonics.* New York: Oxford University Press.

Bayley, R. (2009). *Explicit formal instruction in oral language: English-language learners.* Paper prepared for the Workshop on the Role of Language in School Learning: Implications for Closing the Achievement Gap, October 15-16, Hewlett Foundation, Menlo Park, CA. Retrieved from http://www7.nationalacademies.org/cfe/Paper_Robert_Bayley.pdf

Bennett, C. (2001). Genres of research in multicultural education. *Review of Educational Research, 71*(2), 171-217.

Belfield, C.R. & H.M. Levin, H.M. (2007). *The price we pay: Economic and social consequences of inadequate education.* Washington, DC: Brookins Institution Press.

Bereiter, C., & Englemann, S. (1966). *Teaching disadvantaged children in the preschool.* Englewood Cliffs, NJ: Prentice-Hall.

Berlak, H. (2001). Race and the achievement gap. Retrieved from http://www.rethinkingschools.org/archive/15_04/Race1 54.shtml

Berry III, R. (2003). Mathematics standards, cultural styles, and learning preferences: The plight and the promise of African American students. *Clearing House, 76*(5), 244-249.

Bland-Stewart, L. (2005). Difference or deficit in speakers of African American English. *American Speech-Language-Hearing Association Leader, 10*(6), 6-31.

Boone, P. (2003). When the amen corner comes to class: An examination of the pedagogical and cultural impact of call-response communication in the Black college classroom. *Communication Education, 52*(4), 212–229.

Boykin, A.W. (1986). The triple quandary and the schooling of Afro-American children. In U. Neisser (Ed.), *The school achievement of minority children: New perspectives* (pp. 57-92). Hillsdale, NJ: Erlbaum.

Bronstein, A., Dubner, F., Lee, P., & Raphael, L. (1970). *A socio-linguistic comment on the changing attitudes toward the use of Black English and an experimental study to measure some of those attitudes* (ERIC Document Reproduction Service No. 051-226). New Orleans, LA: Paper presented at the Annual Convention of the Speech Communication Association.

Brown, D. (2004). Urban teachers' professed classroom management strategies: Reflections of culturally responsive teaching. *Urban Education, 39*(3), 266-289.

Bryan, J. & Henry, L. (2008). Strengths-based partnerships: A school-family-community partnership approach to empowering students. *Professional School Counseling, 7*, 162-171.

Burling, R. (1973). *English in black and white.* New York: Holt, Rinehart, and Winston.

Cavazos, L. (2002). Emphasizing performance goals and high-quality education for all students. *Phi Delta Kappan, 83*(9), 690-697.

Cazden, C. (1996). How knowledge about language helps the classroom teacher-or does it? In B. Power & R. Hubbard (Eds.), *Language Development* (pp. 87-100).Englewood Cliffs, NJ: Prentice Hall.

Celious, A., & Oyserman, D. (2001). Race from the inside: An emerging heterogeneous race model. *Journal of Social Issues, 57,* 149-165.

Chambers, J. (2002). Studying language variation: An informal epistemology. In J. K. Chambers, P. Trudgill, and N. Schilling-Estes (Eds.), *The handbook of language variation and change* (pp. 3-12). Oxford, England: Blackwell Publishers, Inc.

Christenbury, L. (2000). *Making the journey: Being and becoming a teacher of English language arts* (2nd ed.). Portsmouth, VA: Boynton/Cook Publishers.

Coe, A. (2006). NAACP works on education equity. *The Crisis, 113*(5), 56.

Coelho, E. (2004). *Adding English: A guide to teaching in multilingual classrooms.* Toronto, Canada: Pippin Publishing.

Commission on Behavioral and Social Sciences and Education. (2002). *Minority students in special and gifted education.* Retrieved from http://books.nap.edu/openbook.php?record_id=10128& page=R1

Connor, C., & Craig, H. (2006). African American preschoolers' language, emergent literacy skills, and use of African American English: A complex relation. *Journal of Speech, Language, and Hearing Research, 49*(4), 771-792.

Conklin, W. (2006). *Instructional strategies for diverse Learners.* Huntington Beach, CA: Shell Education.

Costa, A. & Lowery, L. (1989). *Techniques for teaching thinking.* Pacific Grove, CA: Critical Thinking Press & Software.

Craig, H., Thompson, C., Washington, J., & Potter, S. (2003). Phonological features of child African American English. *Journal of Speech, Language, and Hearing Research, 46,* 623-635.

Craig, H., & Washington, J. (2002). Oral language expectations for African American preschoolers and kindergartners. *American Journal of Speech-Language Pathology, 11,* 59–70.

Craig, H., & Washington, J. (2004). Grade-related changes in the production of African American English. *Journal of Speech, Language, and Hearing Research, 47,* 450–463.

Crawford, J. (2005). *Martin Luther King Junior elementary school children et al. v. Ann Arbor school district.* Retrieved from http://ourworld.compuserve.com/homepages/JWCRAWFORD/king.htm

Csikszentmihalyi, M. & McCormack, J. (1986). The influence of teachers. *Phi Delta Kappan, 67*(1), 415-419.

Cullinan, B. (1974). *Black dialects and reading.* Urbana, IL: National Council of Teachers of English Press.

Cunningham, P. (1976). Teachers' correction responses to Black-dialect miscues which are non-meaning-changing. *Reading Research Quarterly, 12*(4), 637-653.

Cunningham, P., & Allington, R. (1999). (2nd ed.). *Classrooms that work: They can all read and write:* New York: Longman.

Dandy, E. (1991). *Black communications: Breaking down the barriers.* Chicago: African American Images.

Darling-Hammond, L. (2000a). New standards and old inequalities: School reform and the education of African American students. *Journal of Negro Education, 69,* 263–287.

Darling-Hammond, L. (2000b). Teacher quality and student achievement: A review of state policy evidence. *Education Policy Analysis Archives, 8*(1), 31.

Darling-Hammond, L. (2010). *The flat world and education: How America's commitment to equity will determine our future.* New York: Teachers College Press.

Darling-Hammond, L. & Sykes, G. (2003, September 17). Wanted: A national teacher supply policy for education: The right way to meet the "Highly Qualified Teacher" challenge. *Education Policy Analysis Archives, 11*(33).

Darling-Hammond, L. & Youngs, P. (2002). Defining highly qualified teachers: what does scientifically-based research tell us? *Education Researcher, 31*(9), 13-25.

Delpit, L. (1988). The silenced dialogue: Power and pedagogy in educating other people's children. *Harvard Educational Review, 58*(3), 280-297.

Delpit, L. (1995). *Other people's children: Cultural conflicts in the classroom.* New York: New Press.

Delpit, L. (1998). Ebonics and culturally responsive instruction. In T. Perry & L. Delpit (Eds.), *The real Ebonics debate: Power, language, and the education of African American children* (pp.17-26). Boston: Beacon Press.

Delpit, L. (2006). *Other people's children: Cultural conflicts in the classroom.* New York: The New Press.

Dickson, S. V., Simmons, D. C., & Kame'enui, E. J. (1998). Text organization: Research bases. In D. C. Simmons & E. J. Kame'enui (Eds), *What reading research tells us about children with diverse learning needs* (pp. 239-278). Mahwah, NJ: Erlbaum.

Dillard, J. (1972). *Black English: Its history and usage in the United States.* New York: Random House.

Dresser, N. (1996). *Multicultural matters.* New York: John Wiley & Sons.

Dufour, R. (2004). What is a professional learning community? *Educational Leadership, 61*(8), 6-11.

Echevarria, J., Vogt, M., & Short, D.J. (2004). *Making content comprehensible for English learners: The SIOP model* (2nd ed.). Boston: Pearson.

Edens, K. (2000). Preparing problem solvers for the twenty-first century through problem-based learning. *College Teaching, 48*(2), 55–60.

Education Trust. (2003). *African American achievement in America.* Retrieved from http://www2.edtrust.org/NR/rdonlyres/9AB4AC88-7301-43FF-81A3-EB94807B917F/0/AfAmer_Achivement.pdf

Edwards, P., McMillon, G., & Turner, J. (2010). *Change is gonna come: Transforming literacy education for African American students.* New York: Teachers College Press.

Edwards, V. (1997). Patois and politics of protest: Black English in British classrooms. In N. Coupland & A. Jaworski (Eds.), *Sociolinguistics: A reader* (pp.408-15). New York: St. Martin's Press.

Epstein, J., Sanders, M., Simon, B., Salinas, K., Jansorn, N., & Van Voorhis, F. (2002). (2nd ed.). *School, community, and community partnerships: Your handbook for action* Thousand Oaks, CA: Corwin Press.

Farr, B.P. & Trumbull, E. (1997). *Assessment alternatives for diverse classrooms.* Clevedon, UK: Multilingual Matters Ltd.

Fasold, R., & Wolfram, W. (1970). Some linguistics features of Negro dialect. In R. Fasold & R. Shuy (Eds.), *Teaching standard English in the inner city* (pp. 41-86). Washington, DC: Center for Applied Linguistics.

Ferguson, R. (1991). Paying for public education: New evidence on how and why money matters. *Harvard Journal on Legislation, 28*(2), 465-498.

Ferguson, R. (1998). Teachers' perceptions and expectations and black-white test score gap. In C. Jencks & M. Phillips (Eds.), *The black-white test score gap* (pp. 273-317). Washington, DC: Brookings Institution Press.

Ferguson, R. (2006). *The importance of education.* Retrieved from http://www.federalreserve.gov/BoardDocs/Speeches/2006

Fleischman, H.L., Hopstock, P.J., Pelczar, M.P., & Shelley, B.E. (2010). *Highlights from PISA 2009: Performance of U.S. 15-year-old students in reading, mathematics, and science literacy in an international context* (NCES 2011-004). Washington, DC: United States Department of Education, National Center for Education Statistics.

Flowers, D. (2000). Codeswitching and Ebonics in urban adult basic education classrooms. *Education and Urban Society, 32,* 221-236.

Ford, B., Obiakor, F., & Patton, J. (Eds.). (1995). Effective education of African American exceptional learners. Austin, TX: PRO-ED, Inc.

Ford, D., & Harris, J. (1999*). Multicultural gifted education.* New York: Teachers College Press.

Fordham, S. (1996). *Blacked out: Dilemmas of race, identity, and success at Capital High.* Chicago: University of Chicago Press.

Foster, M. (2002). Using call and response to facilitate language mastery and literacy acquisition among African American students. Retrieved from http://www.cal.org/resources/digest/0204foster.html

Fountas, I., & Pinnell, G. (1996). *Guided reading: Good first teaching for all children.* Portsmouth, NH: Heinemann.

Fox, S., & Johnson, J. (2005). Culturally responsive teaching in the world languages classroom. Retrieved from http://www.hamline.edu/gse/diversity_web/summ05_cr t_wrld_lang

Fox, T. (1992). Repositioning the profession: Teaching writing to African American students. Retrieved from http://jac.gsu.edu/jac/12.2/Articles/3.htm

Freire, P. (1998). *Pedagogy of freedom: Ethics, democracy, and civic courage.* Lanham, MD: Rowman & Littlefield Publishers, Inc.

Gall, M., Borg, W., & Gall, J. (1996). *Educational research: An introduction.* White Plains, NY: Longman.

Gardner, H. (1983). Frames of mind: The theory of multiple intelligences. New York: Basic Books.

Gardner, H. (1999). *Intelligence reframed: Multiple intelligences for the 21st century.* New York: Basic Books.

Gardner, H. (2010). Multiple intelligences: The first 25 years with Howard Gardner. Retrieved from http://www.youtube.com/watch?v=tDtZEpf_SJ4&featu re=related

Gay, G. (2000). *Culturally responsive teaching: Theory, research, and practice.* New York: Teachers College Press.

Good, T., & Brophy, J. (2003). *Looking in classrooms* (9th ed.). Boston: Allyn and Bacon.

Goto, S. (1997). Nerds, normal people, and homeboys: Accommodation and resistance among Chinese American students. *Anthropology and Education Quarterly, 28*(1), 70-84.

Green, E. (1999). *A marshland of ethnolinguistic boundaries: Conflicting past and present tense be paradigms in coastal Carolina speech.* (Master's thesis, North Carolina State University, Raleigh, 1999).

Green, L. (1998). Aspect and predicate phrases in African American vernacular English. In S. Mufwene, J. Rickford, G. Bailey, & J. Baugh (Eds.), *African American English: Structure, history, and use* (pp. 37-68). New York: Routledge.

Green, L. (2002a). A descriptive study of African American English: Research in linguistics and education. *Qualitative Studies in Education, 15*(6), 673-690.

Green, L. (2002b). *African-American English: A linguistic introduction.* New York: Cambridge University Press.

Greene, J., & Winters, M. (2005). Public high school graduation and college-readiness rates: 1991-2002. *Education Working Paper, 8,* 1-27.

Hansen, E., & Stephens, J. (2000). The ethics of learner-centered education: Dynamics that impede the process. *Change, 32*(5), 41–47.

Heck, S. (1999). Writing standard English is acquiring a second language: Language alive in the classroom. Westport, CT: Praeger Publishing.

Hoffman, M. (1997). Ebonics: The third incarnation of a thirty-three year old controversy about Black English in the United States. *Links & Letters, 5,* 75-78.

Hoover, J., & Collier, C. (1985). Referring culturally different children: Sociocultural considerations. *Academic Therapy, 20,* 503-509.

Horowitz, J. (2007, February 5). Biden unbound: Lays into Clinton, Obama, Edwards. *New York Observer.* Retrieved from http://www.observer.com/2007/politics/biden-unbound-lays-clinton-obama-edwards

House, G. (2006). *Closing the reality gap.* Retrieved from http://www.asbj.com/specialreports/0406SpecialReports/S4.html

Huitt, W. (2011). Bloom et al.'s taxonomy of the cognitive domain. Retrieved from http://www.edpsycinteractive.org/topics/cognition/bloom.html

Hymes, D. (1974). *Foundations in sociolinguistics.* Philadelphia: University of Pennsylvania Press.

Ibarra, R. (2006). *Context diversity: Reframing higher education in the 21st century.* Retrieved from http://www.compact.org/20th/read/context_diversity

Ingersoll, R. (2007, September). Short on power, long on responsibility. *Educational Leadership, 65*(1), 20-25.

Ingersoll, R., & May, H. (2011, September). The minority teacher shortage: Fact or fable? *Phi Delta Kappan, 93*(1), 62-65.

Isaac, S., & Michael, W. (1995). *Introduction to research in education* (5th ed.). New York: Harcourt Brace College Publishers.

Jax, V. (1988). Understanding school language proficiency through the assessment of story construction. In A. A. Ortiz & B. A. Ramirez (Eds.), *Schools and the culturally diverse exceptional student: Promising practices and future directions* (pp. 45-50). Reston, VA: The Council for Exceptional Children.

Jencks, C. (1972). *Inequality: A reassessment of the effect of family and schooling in America.* New York: Basic Books. Jencks, C., & Phillips, M. (Eds.). (1998). *The black-white test score gap: An introduction.* Washington, DC: Brookings Institute.

Jensen, E. (1998). *Teaching with the brain in mind.* Alexandria, VA: Association for Supervision and Curriculum Development.

Johnson, J. & Duffett, A. (2003). Where we are now: 12 thinks you need to know about public opinion and public schools. New York: Public Agenda.

Johnson, V. (2005). Comprehension of third person singular /s/ in AAE-speaking children. *Language, Speech, and Hearing Services in Schools, 36,* 116-124.

Johnston, M. & Cooley, N. (2001). *Supporting new models of teaching and learning through technology.* Arlington, VA: Educational Research Service.

Jones, A. (2007). Dialectology and oral and written expression: English/language arts teachers' perceptions of Black English usage (Doctoral dissertation). Lamar University, Beaumont.

Kendall, F. (1996). *Diversity in the classroom: New approaches to the education of young children.* New York: Teachers College Press.

Knapp, D. (1996). *Oakland schools adopt 'Black English' policy.* Retrieved from http://www.cnn.com/US/9612/19/black.english/index. html

Koch, L., Gross, A., & Kolts, R. (2001). Attitudes toward Black English and code-switching. *Journal of Black Psychology, 27,* 29-42.

Kochman, T. (1990). Cultural pluralism: black and white styles. In D. Carbaugh (Ed.), *Cultural Communication and Intercultural Context* (pp. 219-224). Hillsdale, NJ: Erlbaum.

Labov, W. (1970). *The study of nonstandard English.* Champaign, IL: National Council of Teachers of English.

Labov, W. (1972). *Language in the inner city: Studies in the Black English vernacular.* Philadelphia: University of Pennsylvania.

Labov, W. (1995). Can reading failure be reversed? *Literacy among African*-American youth: Issues in learning, teaching, and schooling. Cresskill, NJ: Hampton.

Labov, W. (2001). Applying knowledge of the African American English to the problem of raising reading levels in inner-city schools. In S. Lanehart (Ed.), *Sociocultural and Historical Contexts of African American Vernacular* (pp. 299-318). Philadelphia: John Benjamins.

Ladson-Billings, G. (2001). *Crossing over to Canaan.* San Francisco: Jossey-Bass, Inc.

Langdon, H. (1989). Language disorder or difference? Assessing the language skills of Hispanic students. *Exceptional Children, 56,* 160-167.

LeBaron, M. (2003). Communication tools for understanding cultural differences. In Guy Burgess and Heidi Burgess (Eds.), *Beyond Intractability.* Boulder, CO: Conflict Research Consortium, University of Colorado. Retrieved from http://www.beyondintractability.org/essay/communication_tools/

LeMoine, N. (2001). Language variation and literacy acquisition in African American students. In J. L. Harris, A. G. Kamhi, & K. E. Pollock (Eds.), *Literacy in African American communities* (pp. 169–194). Mahwah, NJ: Lawrence Erlbaum Associates, Inc.

Levine, D., & Lezotte, L. (2001). Effective schools research. In J. Banks & C. Banks (Eds.), *Handbook of research on multicultural education* (pp. 525-547). San Francisco: Jossey-Bass.

Linnell, K. (2010). Using dialogue journals to focus on form. *Journal of Adult* Education, 39, 23-28.

Lustig, M., & Koester, J. (2003). *Intercultural competence: Interpersonal communication across cultures.* Boston: Allyn and Bacon.

Machan, T., & Scott, C. (Eds.) (1992). *English in its social contexts: Essays in historical sociolinguistics.* Oxford, England: Oxford University Press.

Martin, S., & Wolfram, W. (1998). The sentence in African American vernacular English. In S. Mufwene, J. Rickford, G. Bailey, & J. Baugh (Eds.), *African American English: Structure, history, and use* (pp. 11-36). New York: Routledge.

155

Matsuda, P. (2006). The myth of linguistic homogeneity in U.S. college composition. *College English, 68*(6), 637-651.

Marzano, R., Pickering, D., & Pollock, J. (2001). *Classroom instruction that works: Research-based strategies for increasing student achievement.* Alexandria, VA: Association for Supervision and Curriculum Development.

Maxim, G. (2006). *Dynamic social studies for constructivist classrooms: Inspiring tomorrow's social scientists.* Columbus, OH: Pearson Merrill Prentice Hall, Inc.

McGinley, W. and Tierney, R. (1989). Traversing the topical landscape: Reading and writing as ways of knowing. *Written Communication, 6,* 243-269.

McIntyre, T. & Battle, J. (1998). The traits of "good teachers" as identified by African American and White students with emotional and/or behavioral disorders. *Behavioral Disorders, 23*(2), 134-142.

Miller, L. (1995). *An American imperative: Accelerating minority educational achievement.* New Haven, CT: Yale University Press.

Minow, M. (2010). *In Brown's wake: Legacies of America's educational landmark.* New York: Oxford University Press.

Moje, E., & Hinchman, K. (2004). Culturally responsive practices for youth literacy learning. In T. L. Jetton & J. A. Dole (Eds.), *Adolescent literacy research and practice* (pp. 321-350). New York: Guilford.

Mufwene, S. (1999). Ebonics and Standard English in the classroom: Some issues. In J. Alatis & A. Tan (Eds.), *Georgetown University Round Table on Languages and Linguistics* (pp. 253-261). Washington, DC: Georgetown University Press.

Mufwene, S., Rickford, J., Bailey, G., & Baugh, J. (Eds.). (1998). *African-American English: Structure, history, and use.* New York: Routledge.

Myers-Scotton, C., & Ury, W. (1977). Bilingual strategies: The social functions of codeswitching. *Linguistics, 19,* 35-20.

Myers-Scotton, C. (2006). *Multiple voices: An introduction to bilingualism.* Malden, MA: Blackwell Publishing.

National Center for Education Statistics. (2010). *Status and trends in the education of racial and ethnic minorities.* Retrieved from http://nces.ed.gov/pubs2010/2010015/indicator3_11.asp

National Center for Education Statistics. (2009a). *Bachelor's degrees conferred by degree-granting institutions, by race/ethnicity and sex of student: Selected years, 1976-77 through 2007-08.* Retrieved from http://nces.ed.gov/programs/digest/d09/tables/dt09_285.asp?referrer=report

National Center for Education Statistics. (2009b). *Educational attainment of persons 25 years old and over, by race/ethnicity and state: 2005-2007.* Retrieved from http://nces.ed.gov/programs/digest/d09/tables/dt09_012.asp

National Center for Education Statistics. (2009c). *The Nation's report card: Grade 12 reading and mathematics 2009 national and state and pilot state results.* Retrieved from http://nces.ed.gov/pubsearch/pubsinfo.asp?pubid=2011455

National Center for Education Statistics. (2011). *Digest of Education Statistics, 2010* (NCES 2011-015). Retrieved from http://nces.ed.gov/FastFacts/display.asp?id=147

National Center for Education Statistics. (2011). *The condition of education 2011(NCES 2011-033).* Retrieved from http://nces.ed.gov/fastfacts/display.asp?id=72

National Council of Teachers of English. (1982). *Non-native and nonstandard dialect students.* Urbana, IL: National Council of Teachers of English.

National Council for Accreditation of Teacher Education. (2010). *Transforming teacher education through clinical practice: A national strategy to prepare effective teachers.* Washington, DC: Author. Retrieved from http://www.ncate.org/Public/ResearchReports/NCATEInitiatives/BlueRibbonPanel/tabid/715/Default.aspx

National Endowment for the Humanities. (2005). *Do you speak American?* Retrieved from http://www.pbs.org/speak/education/curriculum/high/aae/#aaepro

National PTA. (1998). *National standards for parent/family involvement programs.* Chicago, IL: National PTA.

National Research Council. (2010). *Preparing teachers: Building evidence for sound policy*. Committee on the Study of Teacher Preparation Programs in the United States, Center for Education. Division of Behavioral and Social Sciences and Education. Washington, DC: The National Academies Press.

Nieto, S. (1996). *Affirming diversity: The sociopolitical context of multicultural education* (2nd ed.). New York: Longman.

Nieto, S. (1999). *The light in their eyes: Creating multicultural learning communities.* New York: Teachers College Press.

Novick, R. (1996). Developmentally appropriate and culturally responsive education: Theory in practice. Retrieved from http://www.nwrel.org/cfc/publications/DAP2.html#Responsive

Nunnaly, J. (1978). *Psychometric theory.* New York: McGraw-Hill.

Nye, B., Konstantopoulos, S, & Hedges, L.V. (2004, Fall). How large are teacher effects? *Educational Evaluation and Policy Analysis, 26*(3), 237-257.

Ogbu, J. (2003). *Black American students in an affluent suburb: A study of academic disengagement.* Mahwah, NJ: Erlbaum.

Osborne, J. (2001). Unraveling underachievement among African American boys from an identification with academics perspective. *Journal of Negro Education, 68*(4), 555-565.

Oubre, A. (1997). *Black English vernacular (Ebonics) and educability: A cross-cultural perspective on language, cognition, and schooling.* Retrieved from http://www.aawc.com//ebonicsarticle.html

Perie, M., Marion, S., & Gong, B. (2007). *A framework for considering interim assessments.* Retrieved from http://www.nciea.org/publications/ConsideringInterimAssess_M AP07.

Piestrup, A. (1973). *Black dialect interference and accommodation of reading instruction in the first grade.* Berkley, CA: University of California, Language Behavior Research Lab.

Peyton, J. (1993, April). Dialogue journals: Interactive writing to develop language and literacy. Retrieved from F:\CAL Digests Dialogue Journals Interactive Writing to Develop Language and Literacy.htm

Polacco, P. (1994). *Pink and Say*. New York: Philomel Books.

Preston, M. (2010, January 9). Reid apologizes for racial remarks about Obama during campaign. *CNN Politics.* Retrieved from http://articles.cnn.com/2010-01-09/politics/obama.reid_1_john-heilemann-african-american-voters-senator-reid?_s=PM:POLITICS

Pride, J. (Ed.) (1979). *Sociolinguistic aspects of language learning and teaching.* Oxford, England: Oxford University Press.

Reagan, T. (2005). Accents and dialects: Ebonics and beyond. In T. Osborne (Ed.), *Language and cultural diversity in U.S. schools* (pp. 39-50). Westport, CT: Praeger.

Reyes, M. (1992). Challenging venerable assumptions: Literacy instruction for linguistically different students. *Harvard Educational Review, 62*(4), 427-446.

Rickford, J. (1999). *African American vernacular English: Features, evolution, educational implications.* Oxford, England: Blackwell Publishing.

Rickford, J. & Rickford, A. (1995). Dialect readers revisited. *Linguistics and Education, 7*(2), 107-128.

Rickford, J. & Rickford, R. (2000). *Spoken Soul: The story of Black English.* New York: Wiley.

Rickford, J., and Wolfram, W. (2009). *Explicit formal instruction in oral language as a second dialect.* Paper prepared for the Workshop on the Role of Language in School Learning: Implications for Closing the Achievement Gap, October 15-16, Hewlett Foundation, Menlo Park, CA. Retrieved from http://www7.nationalacademies.org/cfe/Paper_Rickford_and_Wolfram.pdf

Rist, R. (2000). Student social class and teacher expectations: Self-fulfilling prophecy in ghetto education. *Harvard Educational Review, 70*(3), 257-301.

Rycik, M. (2002). How primary teachers are using word walls to teach literacy strategies. *Ohio Reading Teacher, 35*(2), 13-20.

Salend, S. (2001). *Creating inclusive classrooms: Effective and reflective practices* (4th ed.). Columbus, OH: Merrill/Prentice Hall.

Sanacore, J. (2004). Genuine caring and literacy learning for African American children. *Reading Teacher, 57*(1), 744-753.

Sanders, W.L., & Rivers, J.C. (1996, November). *Cumulative and residual effects of teachers on future student academic achievement.* Knoxville, TN: University of Tennessee Value-Added Research and Assessment Center.

Schmoker, M. (2006). *Results now: How we can achieve unprecedented improvements in teaching and learning.* Association for Supervision and Curriculum Development. Alexandria, VA.

Scott, C., & Machan, T. (1992). Sociolinguistics, language change, and the history of English. In C.T. Scott and T.W. Machan (Eds.), *English in its social contexts essays in historical sociolinguists* (pp. 3-27). New York: Oxford University Press.

Sealy-Ruiz, Y. (2005). Spoken soul: The language of Black imagination and reality. *The Educational Forum, 70*, 37-45.

Sellers, F. (2012, September 17). Sign language that African Americans use is different from that of whites. *The Washington Post.* Retrieved from http://www.washingtonpost.com/lifestyle/style/sign-language-that-african-americans-use-is-different-from-that-of-whites/2012/09/17/2e897628-bbe2-11e1-8867-ecf6cb7935ef_story.html

Sheldon, S. B. & Epstein, J. L. (2005). School programs of family and community involvement to support children's reading and literacy development across the grades. In J. Flood & P. Anders (Eds.), The literacy development of students in urban schools: Research and policy. Newark, DE: International Reading Association.

Seymour, H., Abdulkarim, L. & Johnson, V. (1999). The Ebonics controversy: An educational and clinical dilemma. *Topics in Language Disorders, 19*(4), 66-77.

Shade, B. & Thomas, C. (1997). African-American cognitive patterns: A review of the research. In C. Thomas & B. Shade (Eds.), *Culture, style and the educative process: Making schools work for racially diverse students* (pp. 70-92). Springfield, IL: Charles C. Thomas Publisher Ltd.

Shuy, R. (1967). *Discovering American dialect.* Champaign, IL: National Council of Teachers of English.

Smith, D. (2003). *Introduction to special education: Teaching in an age of opportunity* (4th ed.). Boston: Allyn & Bacon.

Smith, E. & Crozier, K. (1998). Ebonics is not Black English. *The Western Journal of Black Studies, 22*(2), 109-116.

Smitherman, G. (1977). *Talkin' and testifyin': The language of Black America.* Boston: Houghton Mifflin.

Smitherman, G. (Ed.). (1981). Black English and the education of Black children and Youth, *Proceedings of a National Invitational Symposium on the King Decision.* Detroit, MI: Wayne State University.

Smitherman, G. (1998a). Black English/Ebonics: What it be like? In T. Perry & L. Delpit (Eds.), *The real Ebonics debate: Power, language, and the education of African-American children* (pp. 163-171). Boston: Beacon.

Smitherman, G. (2000). *Talkin that talk: Language culture and education in African America.* New York: Routledge.

Smitherman, G., & Baugh, J. (2002). The shot heard from Ann Arbor: Language research and public policy in African America. *The Howard Journal of Communications, 13,* 5-24.

Snow, C., Burns, S., & Griffin, P. (Eds.). (1998). *Preventing reading difficulties in young children.* Washington, DC: National Academy Press.

Snow, M., & Kamhi-Stein, L. (Eds.) (2006). *Developing a new course for adult learners.* Alexandria, VA: Teachers of English to Speakers to Other Languages, Inc.

Sousa, D. (2011). *How the brain learns* (4th ed.). Thousand Oaks, CA: Corwin Press.

Sprenger, M. (2005). *How to teach so students remember.* Alexandria, VA: ASCD.

Spring, J. (2002). *American education* (10th ed.). New York: McGraw-Hill Companies, Inc.

Spring, J. (2004). *The intersection of cultures.* Boston: McGraw-Hill.

Steele, C. (1997). A threat in the air: How stereotypes shape intellectual identity and performance. *American Psychologist, 52,* 613-629.

Stockman, I. (1996). Phonological development and disorders in African American children. In A. Kamhi, K. Pollock, & J. Harris (Eds.), *Communication development and disorders in African American children* (pp. 117-153). Baltimore: Brookes.

Stubbs, M. (1980). *Language and literacy.* Boston: Routledge & Kegan Paul Ltd.

Sulentic, M. (2001). Black English in a place called Waterloo. *Multicultural Education, 8*(4), 24-30.

Tate, M. (2003). *Worksheets don't grow dendrites: 20 instructional strategies that engage the brain.* Thousand Oaks, CA: Corwin Press.

Taylor, B., Pearson, P., Clark, K., & Walpole, S. (2000). Effective schools and accomplished teachers: Lessons about primary-grade reading instruction in low-income schools. *Elementary School Journal, 101,* 121-165.

Tauber, R. (1997). *Self-fulfilling prophecy: A practical guide to its use in education.* Westport, CT: Praeger Publishers.

Taylor, H. (1989). *Standard English, Black English, and bidialectalism.* New York: Peter Lang Publishing, Inc.

The Language Samples Project. (2001). *Realization of [t,f] and [d,v].* Retrieved from http://www.ic.arizona.edu/~lsp/Features/Realization.html

Thompson, G. (2004). *Through ebony eyes: What teachers need to know but are afraid to ask about African American students.* San Francisco: Jossey-Bass.

Tikunoff, W. (1987). Mediation of instruction to obtain equality of effectiveness. In S. Fradd & W. Tkunoff (Eds.), *Bilinugual education and bilingual special education: A guide for administrators* (pp. 99-132). Boston: Little, Brown and Company.

Tomlinson, C. (2003). Fulfilling the promise of the differentiated classroom: Strategies and tools for responsive teaching. Alexandria, VA: Association for Supervision and Curriculum Development

University of Michigan Digital Library. (2004). *Significant cases: Supreme Court cases.* Retrieved from http://www.lib.umich.edu/exhibits/brownarchive/cases.html#mich5

University of Texas Center for Reading and Language Arts. (2003). *Enhancing reading comprehension for secondary students* (Rev. ed.). Austin, TX: Author.

U.S. Bureau of Labor Statistics. (2010). *African American history month.* Retrieved from http://www.bls.gov/spotlight/2010african_american_his tory/pdf/african_american_spotlight.pdf

U.S. Commission on Civil Rights (2009). *Minorities in special education.* Retrieved from http://www.usccr.gov/pubs/MinoritiesinSpecialEducation.pdf

U.S. Department of Education. (2009a). *The nation's report card: Grade 4 national results.* Retrieved from http://nationsreportcard.gov/reading_2009/nat_g4.asp?s ubtab_id=Tab_3&tab_id=tab1#tabsContainer

U.S. Department of Education. (2009b). *The nation's report card: Grade 8 national results.* Retrieved from http://nationsreportcard.gov/reading_2009/nat_g8.asp?s ubt ab_id=Tab_3&tab_id=tab1#tabsContainer

U.S. Department of Education. (2009c). *The nation's report card: Grade 12 national results.* Retrieved from http://nationsreportcard.gov/reading_2009/gr12_national.asp?sub tab_id=Tab_3&tab_id=tab1#tabsContainer

Valdes, G. (2001). *Learning and not learning English: Latino students in American schools.* New York: Teachers College Press.

Valdez-Pierce, L. (2003). *Assessing English language learners.* Washington, DC: National Education Association.

Van Sertima, I. (1971). African linguistic and mythological structures in the new world. In R.L. Goldstein (Ed.), *Black life and culture in the United States* (pp. 12-35). New York: Thomas Y. Crowell.

Valenzuela, A. (1999). *Subtractive schooling: U.S. Mexican youth and the politics of caring.* Albany, NY: SUNY Press.

Villegas, A., & Lucas, T. (2002). Preparing culturally responsive teachers: Rethinking the curriculum. *Journal of Teacher Education, 53*(1), 20-32.

Washington, G. (1996). The writing crisis in urban schools: A culturally different hypothesis. *JAC: A Journal of Composition Theory, 16*(3), 425-33.

Weaver, C. (1979). *Grammar for teachers: Perspectives and definitions.* Urbana, IL: National Council of Teachers of English.

Weismantel, M. & Fradd, S. (1989). Understanding the need for change. In S. H. Fradd & M. J. Weismantel (Eds.), *Meeting the needs of culturally and linguistically different students: A handbook for educators* (pp.1-13). Boston: Little, Brown and Company.

Wentzel, K. (1997). Student motivation in middle school: The role of perceived pedagogical caring. *Journal of Educational Psychology, 89*, 411-419.

Wheeler, R. (2005). Teaching English in the world. *English Journal, 94*(5), 108-112.

Wheeler, R. & Swords, R. (2006). *Code-switching: Teaching standard English in urban classrooms.* Urbana: National Council of Teachers of English.

Whiteman, M. (1976). *Dialect influence and the writing of African American and white working class Americans.* (Unpublished doctoral dissertation, Georgetown University, Washington, DC, 1976).

Wiersma, W. & Jurs. (2005). *Research methods in education: An introduction* (8th ed.). Boston: Allyn and Bacon.

Williams, P. (2001). The hidden meanings of Black English. *Black Scholar, 27*(1), 7.

Wisconsin Department of Public Instruction. (2005). *SAT scores up, state's graduates among tops in the nation.* Retrieved from http://dpi.state.wi.us/eis/pdf/dpi2005_114.pdf

Wisconsin Center for Education Research (2009). *WIDA focus on formative assessement.* Retrieved from http://www.wida.us/Resources/focus/Bulletin2.pdf

Witkosky, D. (2005). The road to bidialectalism in American and German schools: 1960-2004. *American Educational History Journal, 32*(1), 20-27.

Wolfram, W. (2000). Issues in reconstructing earlier African-American English. *World Englishes, 19*(1), 39-58.

Wolfram, W., Adger, C., & Christian, D. (1999). *Dialects in schools and communities.* Mahwah, NJ: Erlbaum.

Wolfram, W. & Beckett, D. (2000). The role of the individual and group in earlier African American English. *American Speech, 75*(1), 3-33.

Wong-Fillmore, L., & Snow, C. (2000). What teachers need to know about language. In C.A. Adger, C. E. Snow, & D. Christian (Eds.), *What teachers need to know about language* (pp.7-54). Washington, DC: Center for Applied Linguistics.

Wright, A., & Saks, J. (2000). *The community connection: Case studies in public engagement.* Alexandria, VA: National School Boards Association.

Wrigley, P. (2000). Educating English language learners in rural areas. *National Association for Bilingual Education News, 24*(2), 10-13.

Yates, J. (1998, April). *The state of practice in the education of CLD students.* Presentation at the annual meeting of the Council for Exceptional Children, Minneapolis, MN.

Youngs, C., & Youngs, G. (2001). Predictors of mainstream teachers' attitudes toward ESL students. *Teachers of English to Speakers of Others Languages (TESOL), Quarterly, 35*(1), 97-118.

Zeigler, M., & Osinubi, V. (2002). Theorizing the postcoloniality of African American English. *Journal of Black Studies, 32*(5), 588-609.

Zeleny, J. (2010). Reid apologizes for remarks on Obama's color and 'dialect.' Retreived from http://www.nytimes.com/2010/01/10/us/politics/10reidweb.html

Zull, J. (2002). *The art of changing the brain: Enriching teaching by exploring the biology of learning.* Sterling Virginia: Stylus.

Zull, J. (2004). The art of changing the brain. *Educational Leadership, 62*(1), 68-72.

Appendix A: Survey Instrument

English/Language Arts Teachers' Perceptions of Black English Usage Survey

I understand that the return of my completed survey constitutes my informed consent to act as a participant in this research.

Directions: This survey contains three sections: 1) demographic information, 2) Likert-type questions, 3) one fixed response question and three open-ended questions. Please participate by selecting the appropriate response to each question **according to your past and/or present experiences as a teacher of English/language arts. DO NOT** place your name on this survey.

Purpose: To investigate English/Language arts teachers' perceptions regarding Black English usage in students' oral and written expression

Definition of Black English (BE): A systematic, rule-governed dialect of Standard English, used by some (but not all) African Americans, as well as others who are not African American (Bland-Stewart, 2005).

Definition of Standard English (SE): The middle-class, educated, language variety associated with native speakers of a region (Wolfram & Schilling-Estes, 1998).

PART I

Please complete questions **1, 3-7** by placing a check (√) or an (X) in front of the **one** most appropriate response. For question **#2**, please write your age legibly.

1) **Ethnicity**

   ____Asian ____Black ____Hispanic ____Native American ____White

   ____Other (specify____)

2) **Age**

   _____

3) **Highest Level of Education**

   ____Bachelor's Degree

   ____Graduate Degree

4) **Gender**

   ____Female

   ____Male

5) **Years of Experience as Educator**

   ____1-15 years ____16+ years

6) I have received instruction/training in non-standard English dialects.

_____Yes   _____No

7) Grade level(s) taught

_____Elementary (PK-6)   _____Secondary (7-12)   _____All levels

Part II. **Please rate your level of agreement (from 0-4) with each of the following statements by circling ONE most appropriate rating.**

Strongly Disagree   **Strongly Agree**

       0   1   2   3   4

8. I am very familiar with Black English (BE) (a non-standard English dialect).

       0   1   2   3   4

9. I find it challenging to teach writing composition to Black English (BE)-speaking students.

       0   1   2   3   4

10. I find it more difficult to teach writing composition to BE-speaking students than other students.

       0   1   2   3   4

11. I am able to communicate well with BE-speaking students.

       0   1   2   3   4

12. I have a strong rapport with BE-speaking students.

       0   1   2   3   4

13. I clearly understand BE-speaking students' colloquial syntax (everyday speech).

       0   1   2   3   4

14. I often correct BE-speaking students' speech during informal discussions (outside of class).

       0   1   2   3   4

15. I often correct BE-speaking students' speech during formal/class discussions.

       0   1   2   3   4

16. I feel it is necessary to constantly correct BE-speaking students during class discussions.

       0   1   2   3   4

17. I feel it is necessary to constantly correct BE-speaking students during writing instruction.

       0   1   2   3   4

18. It is important to correct BE-speaking students each time they mispronounce a word during reading time.

       0   1   2   3   4

167

19. I correct BE-speaking students' writing each time they use non-standard English in written composition.

    0   1   2   3   4

20. BE-speaking students become frustrated when corrected for incorrect use of Standard English (SE) in writing.

    0   1   2   3   4

21. BE-speaking students often become frustrated when corrected for incorrect oral use of SE.

    0   1   2   3   4

22. BE-speaking students should be encouraged to use only Standard English at and away from school.

    0   1   2   3   4

Part III. Please respond briefly to each of the following questions (You may use the back of this sheet if you need extra space).

23. The following list supplies common examples of Black English features. Please place a check mark beside the **three** features you have observed **most frequently** in Black-English speaking students' writing.

    _____A.) "She _ my teacher."   (missing verb)

    _____B) "He *be* working."

    _____C) "He *been* working."

    _____D) "Yesterday, I *wash* my car."

    _____E) "I drove down the *skreet.*"

    _____F) "She *like* to read."

    _____G) "My *teacher* pencil broke."

    _____H) "He *done* finished his homework."

    _____I) "*Dey* already left."

    _____J) "My dog took a *baf.*

    _____K) "Nobody *don't want none.*"

PLEASE CONTINUE TO NEXT PAGE

24. List any specific concerns you have with regard to teaching BE-speaking students to speak or write in Standard English.

25. What professional development would you find helpful for teaching BE-speaking students Standard English?

26. What advice would you give beginning teachers that would be most helpful when teaching Standard English to BE-speaking students?

Thank you for taking the time to complete this survey.

Appendix B: Supplements to Research Study

Overview of the Problem

One of the most challenging issues for English/language arts (ELA) teachers is their responsibility to students who speak nonstandard English (Christenbury, 2000). Research enveloping Black English (BE) dialect has focused primarily on the overall structure of Black English, as well as BE speakers' use of the language in social contexts. Although advocates of Black English have attempted to promote the authenticity of the language, others have tried to denounce the dialect as having any legitimacy (Baugh, 2000; Green, 2002a; Johnson, 2005; Labov, 1972; Mufwene et al., 1998; Smitherman, 2000).

Despite numerous studies on Black English, Green (2002a) asserted that limited linguistic studies have focused on the effect of language use of child [Black English] speakers on achievement in language arts. Reagan (2005) explained that the national debate surrounding Black English is an educational concern, essentially focused on the most appropriate means of meeting the academic needs of its speakers. The study augmented this research base by exploring the perceptions of English/language arts teachers who are confronted daily with the intricacies of Black English dialect and BE-speaking students' cultural and linguistic differences.

Purpose Statement

The purpose of this research was to determine the perceptions of English/language arts teachers concerning Black English usage in students' oral and written expression.

Research Questions

Eleven research questions guided the study. Quantitative questions examined English/language arts teachers' demographic (or independent) variables across three dependent grouping variables, or clusters. The independent variables included: (a) ethnicity, (b) age, (c)

170

highest level of education, (d) gender, (e) years of experience as an educator, (f) academic training in nonstandard English dialects, and (g) grade level(s) taught. Dependent grouping variables (or clusters) included: (a) communicative competence regarding Black English, (b) challenge of teaching Standard English to Black English speakers, and (c) importance of constant correction of Black English usage.

Other research questions focused on ELA teachers' perceptions regarding: (a) the three most common BE features evidenced in BE-speaking students' writing, (b) concerns with regard to teaching BE-speaking students to speak or write in Standard English, (c) useful professional development for teaching Standard English to Black English-speaking students, and (d) advice for beginning teachers that would be helpful when teaching Standard English to BE-speaking students.

Significance of the Study

This study sought to investigate English/language arts teachers' perceptions regarding Black English usage in students' oral and written expression. This research may be significant in that it revisited the language arts classroom after over 30 years of sociolinguistic discourse. The research was designed to assist educational leaders in better meeting the needs of Black English-speaking students and other Standard English language learners.

Results from the study may raise the level of awareness of how English/language arts teachers perceive Black English dialect to impact students' oral and written expression in the English/language arts classroom. Educators and policymakers may be able to use findings from the study to expand their knowledge base concerning ELA teachers' overall perceptions of Black English usage as well as specific concerns and recommendations with regard to teaching Black English speakers.

Foundational Assumptions

Foundational assumptions for the study included the following: (a) The study participants provided open and honest responses to the self-assessment survey, considering the volunteerism and anonymity of the instrument, (b) the study participants' membership in the National Council of Teachers of English (NCTE) provided an adequate level of homogeneity within the sample population, and (c) the English/language arts teachers responding to the survey were similar on relevant variables to those who taught BE speakers but did not participate in the study.

Limitations and Delimitations

While surveys are widely used in education, they are not without limitations. Isaac and Michael (1995) noted that although surveys are often the most cost-effective, efficient, and credible means of collecting data, they are reactive methods that run the risk of generating misleading information by:

1. Making the respondent feel special or unnatural and thus produce responses that are artificial or slanted.

2. Arousing response sets such as the tendency to agree with positive statements.

3. Possessing over-rater or under-rater bias, or the tendency to give consistently high or low ratings.

4. Collecting data at only one point in time. (p. 137)

Study Limitations

In addition to the previous types of limitations, mailed questionnaires run the risk of yielding low response rates. Because low response rates are among the greatest concerns regarding mail surveys, follow-up surveys are paramount (Ary, Jacobs, & Razavieh, 1996; Wiersma & Jurs, 2005). However, the National Council of Teachers of English outlined specific guidelines for use of membership information, including a prohibition to photocopy membership addresses. This guideline limited the researcher to one-time use of each mailing address, which precluded the researcher from conducting follow-ups.

Survey research traditionally has a low response rate of return, which may affect the sample integrity of the target populations. Nonresponse error may theoretically occur if anything less than a 100% response rate is collected, or when researchers fail to collect data from each member of the sample (Wiersma & Jurs, 2005). According to Ary, Jacobs, and Razavieh (1996), low response rates negatively affect the validity of the researcher's results because those who responded may represent a self-selected group that is not representative of the entire target population. The calculated response rate for this study reflected 16.1%. Some ELA teachers returned incomplete surveys, indicating that they had never taught Black English speakers. This indication may explain why other ELA teachers failed to respond to the survey, thus contributing to the low response rate.

Study Delimitations

The researcher limited the sample population in the study to teachers who currently teach or previously taught English/language arts. The results of the study may not generalize to teachers of other subjects. This delimitation did not flaw the study because the researcher was primarily interested in the perceptions of teachers who had experience in teaching English/language arts to Black English-speaking students. Additionally, the participants were adults who earned at least a bachelor's degree.

Research Design

The research methodology for this study reflected a non-experimental descriptive research design, using survey methodology. The researcher developed a questionnaire entitled, *English/Language Arts Teachers' Perceptions of Black English Usage Survey* based upon research literature enveloping Black English usage. Following a pilot of the instrument, the researcher revised the questionnaire.

Bartlett's Test of Sphericity and Kaiser-Meyer-Olkin (KMO) validity analyses revealed significance and adequacy for each cluster. According to the principal axis factor analysis, three eigenvalues emerged that were greater than one and accounted for over 40% of the variance for each cluster, indicating a good result.

The utilization of factor analysis revealed an overall reliability alpha of 0.70 for the survey questionnaire. In addition, the reliability coefficients for each of the three clusters included: (a) a reliability alpha of 0.82 for the *Communicative Competence Regarding Black English* cluster, (b) a reliability alpha of 0.69 for the *Challenge of Teaching Standard English to Black English Speakers* cluster, and (c) a reliability alpha of 0.84 for the *Importance of Constant Correction of Black English Usage* cluster.

Data Collection and Analysis Procedures

The researcher mailed copies of the revised survey questionnaire to a purposive sample of 600 English/language arts teachers across the United States, members of the National Council of Teachers of English (NCTE). Out of 545 surveys used, 88 participants completed and returned the 26-item questionnaire, which reflected a response rate of 16.1%. Because of the NCTE guideline requesting one-time use of membership mailing lists, the researcher was not allowed to reuse the mailing lists for follow-up procedures.

The researcher used the 12.0 version of the *Statistical Package for the Social Sciences* (SPSS 12.0) software program to input and analyze quantitative data. The utilization of frequencies, means, and standard deviations provided descriptive analyses of data. For inferential statistics, one-way analysis of variance (ANOVA) and Mann-Whitney U tests measured interactions of variables, analyzing each independent variable across each dependent grouping variable, or cluster. Data reduction through the use of coding and categorization techniques allowed the researcher to identify emergent themes in open-ended responses, or qualitative data.

Appendix C: Balanced Literacy Components

Balanced Literacy Instructional Framework

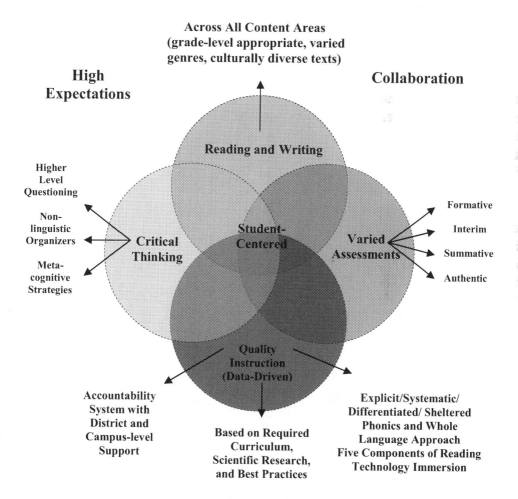

Across All Content Areas
(grade-level appropriate, varied
genres, culturally diverse texts)

**High
Expectations**

Collaboration

Higher
Level
Questioning

Non-
linguistic
Organizers

Meta-
cognitive
Strategies

Reading and Writing

Critical
Thinking

Student-
Centered

Varied
Assessments

Formative

Interim

Summative

Authentic

Quality
Instruction
(Data-Driven)

Accountability
System with
District and
Campus-level
Support

Based on Required
Curriculum,
Scientific Research,
and Best Practices

Explicit/Systematic/
Differentiated/ Sheltered
Phonics and Whole
Language Approach
Five Components of Reading
Technology Immersion

175

Key Components of a Comprehensive Literacy Program

Components (A-G)	Level (check one)				Score (1-4)
A. Classroom Environment/Organization	**1**	**2**	**3**	**4**	
Classroom climate communicates high expectations.					
Reading/ELA objectives are clearly posted in classroom for students.					
Reading/writing materials are readily available.					
Bulletin boards/resources (word walls, etc.) are meaningful, attractive, and current.					
Classroom arrangement is conducive to lesson mastery.					
Students are accustomed to routines (structured environment).					
Quality student work is displayed.					
Print-rich environment with student and teacher resources (clear labels, classroom libraries/centers, etc.)					
Average					
B. Instructional Methodology					
Reading instruction reflects implementation of core curriculum.					
Introduction of lesson sets purpose for reading/writing and engages students in meaningful activities.					
Instructional approach is explicit, systematic, and supports stated objective(s).					
Instruction involves both reading and writing activities.					
Adequate pacing is evident.					
Literature is at the heart of reading program.					

Instructional Methodology cont'd	1	2	3	4	Score
Skills and strategies are taught explicitly with teacher modeling and scaffolding.					
Reading instruction targets word recognition and identification, vocabulary, fluency, and comprehension.					
Writing instruction involves learning to express meaningful ideas, using conventional spelling, grammar, and punctuation.					
Students use reading and writing as tools for learning in the content areas.					
Cooperative groups are implemented.					
Balance of whole group and small group instruction is evident.					
Technology is immersed in instructional modules.					
Students are actively involved in the reading process: **Pre-reading**, **Reading**, **Responding** (response journals/logs), **Exploring** (thinking deeply and making connections: text-to-self, text-to-world, text-to-text), **Applying** (students apply strategies during independent reading).					
All students are afforded opportunities to engage in meaningful reading and writing experiences:					
o Shared (with partner/buddy)					
o Interactive (e.g., read-aloud; choral reading, reader's theatre; writing—"sharing the pen")					
o Guided (with teacher in small groups)					
o Independent/self-selected (e.g., reading center/reader's workshop; writing center)					
Average					

Components	1	2	3	4	Score
C. Study Skills					
Students utilize study skills to organize textual information and stimulate thought processes such as:					
o Skimming/scanning/previewing text					
o Paraphrasing					
o Note-taking					
o Following directions					
o Using non-linguistic organizers (e.g., graphic organizers) to organize ideas.					
Average					
D. Assessment/Progress Monitoring					
Assessment is directly linked to lesson objective(s).					
Ongoing assessment/progress monitoring drives instructional practices.					
Students are provided appropriate practice opportunities that directly reflect instruction/skill mastery: responses to questions, exit tickets, quizzes, authentic assessments, etc.					
Application and transfer of knowledge to other content and real life is assessed.					
Average					
E. Differentiated Instruction					
All reading/writing levels are addressed.					
Reading and writing instruction allows for student choice.					
Instructional framework allows success for all.					
Student literacy center work promotes skill mastery for all students.					
Diverse learning styles/reading levels are addressed.					
Average					

178

Components	1	2	3	4	Score
F. Content					
Materials and strategies are age appropriate.					
Content-appropriate for mastery of targeted skills.					
A variety of genres and topics is provided.					
Average					
G. Cognitive Domain					
Teachers model and students engage in meta-cognitive/think-aloud strategies for increased comprehension (e.g., SQ3R, visual think-alouds).					
Higher-level questioning fosters critical thinking: (e.g., Why do you think the character. . .? What do you predict will happen next? What would you have done differently to solve the problem? Why?)					
Students use non-linguistic organizers (e.g., Frayer Model) to promote critical thinking.					
Average					

Indicators:

Level 1: Unsatisfactory—No Evidence
Level 2: Basic—Some or Limited Evidence
Level 3: Proficient—Satisfactory Evidence
Level 4: Exceeds Expectations—Extensive Evidence

Overall Campus Rating (check one):

- ○ **Unsatisfactory**

- ○ **Basic**

- ○ **Proficient**

- ○ **Exceeds Expectations**

Comment(s):

_____

_____

_____

_____

_____

_____

_____

_____

INDEX

E

Education Trust, 25, 26
English as a second language (ESL), 107
English language cueing systems, 1
    phonological, 1
    pragmatic, 1
    semantic, 1
    syntactic, 1
English language learners (ELLs), 107
Expressive individualism. *See* African
    American cultural experience (nine
    dimensions)

F

Fader, Dan, 9
Flossie and the Fox (McKissack), 114
Frayer Model, 123, 124

G

Game Change (Heilemann and Halperin),
    5
Gardner, Howard, 128
Gifted and talented programs
    and minority students, 25
Graduation rates, 28
Grammar, 2, 7, 12, 38, 98
    defined, 43

H

Habitual *be*, 14
Halperin, Mark, 5
Harmony. *See* African American cultural
    experience (nine dimensions)
Heilemann, John, 5
Higher order thinking, 118

I

Interactive writing, 117
International Reading Association, 134

J

Joiner, Charles, 9
Journaling, 115

K

Key components of a comprehensive
    literacy program, 176

L

Labov, William, 9, 11
Language
    diversity, 3, 10
    variation, 3, 7, 11, 12, 13, 41
Learning objectives, 107, 108, 122, 130
LeMoine, Noma, 111
Linguistically diverse learners, 13, 19, 29,
    30, 105
Linguistics, 19, 137
Literacy, 20, 111, 112, 114
Literacy program. See Key components of
    a comprehensive literacy program

M

Martin Luther King Junior Elementary
    School Children v. Ann Arbor School
    District, 9
Marzano's nine high probability
    instructional strategies, 114
Maslow, Abraham, 120
McCaskill, Carolyn, 39
McKissack, Patricia, 114
Meta-cognitive strategies, 127, 128
Mnemonic devices, 121
Movement. *See* African American cultural
    experience (nine dimensions)
Multiple intelligences, 128
Mutual intelligibility, 1
Myers-Scotton, Carol, xiv

N

National Assessment of Educational
    Progress (NAEP)
    reading scores, 26
National Center for Education Statistics, 6,
    25, 28
National Council for Accreditation of
    Teacher Education (NCATE), 134
National Endowment for the Humanities, 8
National Research Council, 135

Negative concord, 18
Negative polarity items (NPIs), 18
Non-linguistic representations, 114, 123
Nonstandard English, 8, 11, 12, 48, 51, 54,
79, 90, 95, 96, 100, 102, 105, 171
defined, 43

O

Oakland Controversy, 10
Obama, Barack, 5, 143
Orality. *See* African American cultural
experience (nine dimensions)
Other People's Children (Delpit), 33

P

Participatory entry, 35
Performance-based assessments, 110
Piestrup, Ann McCormick, 36
Pink and Say (Polacco), 127
Polacco, Patricia, 127
Professional learning communities (PLCs)
guiding principles, 139
Programme for International Student
Assessment (PISA), 143

R

Race to the Top (RTTT), 143
Reading instruction, 36, 112, 113
constructivist theory, 112
interactive theory, 112
reader response theory, 113
sociolinguistic theory, 112
Reid, Harry, 5
Rubrics, 110

S

S.O.F.T. evaluation tool, 36
Scholastic Aptitude Test (SAT), 27
Second language teaching and African
American learners, 111
Self-fulfilling prophecies, 21
Sharing the pen. *See* Interactive writing
Sheltered English Instruction, 107
Sheltered Instruction Observation Protocol
(SIOP), 107
Signification, 34

Smitherman, Geneva, 9, 117
Social perspective of time. *See* African
American cultural experience (nine
dimensions)
Sociolinguistics, 3
Sound-spelling correspondences, 16
Sousa, David, 122
Special education
and African American students, 25
Speech walls, 126
Spirituality. *See* African American cultural
experience (nine dimensions)
Sprenger, Marilee, 121
Stakeholders, 138, 139, 140
Standard English
defined, 43
speakers, 5, 8, 12, 13, 14, 84
Standard English language learners, 111
Student-centered instruction, 32
Subject-verb disagreement and suffix -*s*, 18
Substitutions in Black English. *See* Black
English: phonological features

T

Talkin' that Talk (Smitherman), 14
Teacher attitudes, 20
Teacher attrition, 138
Teacher modeling, 108, 121, 127
Teacher perceptions, 20
English/language arts teachers, 42
Teacher-centered instruction, 32
Tompkins, Gail, 1

V

V.I.N.E. L.I.M.B.S.S.. See Multiple
intelligences
Verbal deprivation theory, 11
Verbal/aspectual markers, 14
Verve. *See* African American cultural
experience (nine dimensions)

W

West African languages, 8
White teachers, 20
Williams, Robert, 7
Word walls, 126
Writing, 111, 114

183